KIDS GONE WILD

Kids Gone Wild

From Rainbow Parties to Sexting,
Understanding the Hype Over Teen Sex

Joel Best and Kathleen A. Bogle

NEW YORK UNIVERSITY PRESS
New York and London

NEW YORK UNIVERSITY PRESS
New York and London
www.nyupress.org

References to Internet websites (URLs) were accurate at the time of writing.
Neither the author nor New York University Press is responsible for URLs
that may have expired or changed since the manuscript was prepared.

Library of Congress Cataloging-in-Publication Data
Best, Joel.
Kids gone wild : from rainbow parties to sexting, understanding the hype
over teen sex / Joel Best and Kathleen A. Bogle.
pages   cm
Includes bibliographical references and index.
ISBN 978-0-8147-6073-4 (hardback)
1. Teenagers—Sexual behavior. 2. Teenagers in mass media. 3. Sex in
mass media.   I. Bogle, Kathleen A. II. Title.
HQ27.B47 2014
306.70835—dc23   2014015121

New York University Press books are printed on acid-free paper,
and their binding materials are chosen for strength and durability.
We strive to use environmentally responsible suppliers and materials
to the greatest extent possible in publishing our books.

Manufactured in the United States of America

10 9 8 7 6 5 4 3 2 1

Also available as an ebook

CONTENTS

Twenty-year-old singer/actress Miley Cyrus's performance on MTV's 2013 Video Music Awards made headlines around the world. Cyrus, who became a teen sensation by starring in the Disney series *Hannah Montana* from 2006 to 2011, was widely criticized for "twerking" her sexually charged dance moves. Wikipedia defines *twerking* as "a type of dancing in which the dancer, usually a woman, shakes her hips in an up-and-down bouncing motion, causing the dancer's buttocks to shake, 'wobble' and 'jiggle.' . . . To twerk is to dance to popular music in a sexually provocative manner involving thrusting hip movements and a low squatting stance." This performance made headlines around the world:

> "Miley Cyrus Twerkfest Sparks Cultural Freakout" — *USA Today*
> "Teen Culture Run Amok" — *Washington Post*
> "Miley, a Role Model No More for Young" — *New Straits Times* (Malaysia)
> "The Blurry Line between Sex and Sexploitation" — *Daily Telegraph* (Australia)
> "What This Twerk Tells Us about the Pornification of Our Children" — *Daily Mail* (England)

Cyrus was not the first pop artist to push sexual boundaries onstage, so why did her performance touch such a nerve? It appears that Miley twerked into adults' fears that today's kids have gone wild.

This twerking scandal is just one example of the media's fascination with stories about wantonly sexual kids in recent years. We have
been told that schoolchildren are using sex bracelets to initiate sexual
encounters, that junior high schoolers are attending rainbow parties,
that high school students are not just sexting but also forming pregnancy pacts, and so on. But a closer look at these stories may tell us
more about *what adults fear* than about what kids and teens are *actually
doing* sexually. What has us so scared?

Much of the concern seems to be about girls. Some people worry
that popular culture icons, such as Miley Cyrus, are a corrupting influence on their young female fans. Thus, we hear lots of discussion in the
media about the bad examples set for impressionable kids when celebri-
ties such as Britney Spears, Lindsay Lohan, and Paris Hilton, fall from
grace. Pundits also point to the detrimental effect of sexually explicit
content in movies, television shows, music, and video games aimed at
kids. While some commentators view girls as victims of a misogynis-
tic culture and worry about them being exploited sexually, others put a
different spin on things and suggest that there has been a fundamental
change in the character and morality of girls. They are troubled by the
behavior of girls today who are doing things, in their view, that girls
of yesteryear would not have dreamt of doing. They worry that behavior that was once limited to girls from the wrong side of the tracks has
come to characterize mainstream America. The focus of reports about
sex-crazed girls has been on white, middle-class, girl-next-door types,
and the message is clear: it isn't just *other* girls behaving badly; it might
be *your* kid, too.[1]

In some ways, media coverage about kids and sex can be justified
for capturing the sentiments of a public that is deeply troubled about
our youth. In other words, journalists are simply reporting what people
are talking about—and people today are worried about the sexuality
of young people, especially girls. However, it is not just the amount of
coverage that teen sex receives but the ways the media—particularly
television—present the story. Their stories are rarely hard news pieces,

products of thorough investigative reporting, or at least interviews with experts who have actually conducted research; rather, TV usually opts for discussing teen sex in an "infotainment" format. For example, NBC's top-rated *Today Show* ran a piece in 2008 about teen sex that featured host Matt Lauer interviewing model-turned-television-talk-show-host Tyra Banks.[2] The piece discussed the results of a survey of young women conducted by *The Tyra Banks Show*, a nonscientific, unrepresentative online survey of 10,000 of the show's viewers. Lauer set up the interview: "If you're the parent of a teenage girl, you may want to sit down right about now. . . . The average age girls are losing their virginity: 15 years old." This was followed by a clip from *The Tyra Banks Show* featuring an exchange between Banks and one of the teenagers she interviewed among a panel of eight girls:

BANKS: How many partners have you had?

GUEST: I've had nine partners.

BANKS: Nine partners. And how old are you?

GUEST: Sixteen.

BANKS: Sixteen years old, with nine partners? How old were you when you lost your virginity?

GUEST: Thirteen.

BANKS: Thirteen years old?

GUEST: Yeah.

BANKS: Wow!

The interview then proceeded with a discussion of the survey's shocking findings, including the percentages of teens having sex while at school and of girls who want to be teen moms.

An astute viewer may have been skeptical of the dubious survey's results. However, the majority of people who watched this segment and consider NBC a reliable source of information may have been unable to discern how much of it was done for entertainment and promotional value (Banks was promoting both her show and *The Clique*—a movie from her production company based on a teen novel). And Lauer ended the segment with an endorsement: "Keep doing surveys like this and keep coming around to talk about the results of these surveys, because it's important."

The Today Show's coverage of teen sex illustrates the trend toward tabloidization of the news, with stories becoming more sensationalized and the press more focused on commercial considerations. The media choose how to frame the stories they run, so that we receive a selective viewpoint of any topic, not a "mirror of reality." In fact, "newsworthy" stories tend to capture the exceptions, not the norm: "If the weather report paid as much attention to sunny, mild days as it did to hurricanes, floods, heat waves, and cold spells, it might be a more accurate representation of the weather, but it would no longer be news."[3]

When it comes to stories on kids and sex, media executives could opt to present an academic analysis, which might give a more complete picture of the subject. Instead, with ratings in mind, their stories tend to be covered in a way that surprises, excites, and is tailored to appeal to the widest audience. Typical reports feature some shocking event and claim that it is a trend among average kids, one that is sweeping the nation. This is not a new phenomenon—warning white, middle-class parents about dangers teen sex poses to them and their children has been a news program staple for decades. For example, in the 1980s, the news was inundated with stories warning parents about the risk of kids contracting HIV/AIDS. More recently, we have been assured that hooking up, friends with benefits, and sexting are ubiquitous. These reported "epidemics" among white, middle-class kids have more to do with television ratings and selling newspapers than a balanced analysis of a given issue.

The question is, if the coverage of teen sex has been misleading (or at least giving an incomplete picture of what is going on), is it distorting public perception and exacerbating people's fears? One recent survey by the Campaign to Prevent Teen and Unplanned Pregnancy found that most Americans believe teen pregnancy has gone up since 1990, when, in fact, teen pregnancies and births have decreased by over 40% during that period.[4] When you combine the media's propensity to sell scare stories about kids with a public ripe to hear them, narratives about sex bracelets, rainbow parties, and sexting can get a lot of traction. As it turns out, it is not only Americans who are concerned about kids today; each of these topics has received considerable media attention around the globe. This book will analyze what all the fuss is about.

ACKNOWLEDGMENTS

Several colleagues helped with this project. In addition to suggesting ideas, they also helped us track the sex-bracelet and rainbow-party stories in other countries. In addition to Chelsea Johnstone, who assisted us in the early data collection, we want to thank Jun Ayukawa, Tjalling Beetstra, Eric Best, Peter Burger, Brian Chapman, Robert Dingwall, Bill Ellis, Whitney Gunter, Elissa R. Henken, Martin Horbach, Changeog Huh, Kathleen Lewis, Carl Lindahl, Suzanne Lipovsky, Robert Macgregor, Marco Marzana, Hayley Reese, Rodrigo Saad, Eric Tranby, and Elizabeth Tucker. And a special thanks to Jeanne Benedict for her feedback throughout the writing process.

Parts of chapters 1 and 2 appeared in an earlier version as Joel Best, Kathleen A. Bogle, and Chelsea Johnstone, "The Shag-Band Menace: Tracing the Spread of a Contemporary Legend," *Symbolic Interaction* 35 (2012): 403–20.

1

These Kids Today

Hold on to your underwear for this one.
—Michelle Burford on *Oprah*, 2003

Most of us—parents in particular—try to protect children from sexual dangers. The last two decades of the twentieth century featured intense, heavily publicized campaigns against pedophiles, child pornographers, and other bad guys who sexually menaced innocent, vulnerable young people.[1] But as the new millennium began, the focus seemed to shift. People talked less about stranger danger and more about the sexual threats young people posed *to themselves*. From rainbow parties to sex bracelets to sexting, kids seemed to be going wild. What, the media repeatedly asked, were average parents supposed to do to keep their children safe from licentious debauchery? Of course, this was hardly a new theme; late twentieth-century commentators worried about reducing teen pregnancy and encouraging safe sex, just as previous generations had tried to supervise courtship and going steady. But there was a new fascination with the dangers posed by ever younger people—even elementary school students—engaging in apparently new, often so shocking that they could not be named, sexual practices.

These concerns focused on threats to children's innocence. Each focused on a different age group, from children in elementary school to teens in high school.

Sex Bracelets

Children in primary school were reported to be wearing *sex bracelets*. Also known as shag bands,[2] gel bracelets, and jelly bracelets,[3] these were a child's fashion accessory. They were inexpensive, thin, o-ring bracelets, made from a supple plastic gel, sold in a variety of colors, and most often worn by grade school and junior high school children, usually girls. The bracelets first became popular in the 1980s, when they were featured in Madonna and Cindi Lauper videos. Then, beginning in 2003, they gained new notoriety with warnings linking them to sexual behavior, with different colored bands said to represent different sexual acts, ranging from the relatively innocent (hugging, kissing) to some that seemed shocking (fisting, analingus). There were three major stories about the bracelets' meanings: (1) bracelets' colors signified which sexual acts the wearer had already performed; (2) bracelets' colors signified which sexual acts the wearer was willing to perform; or, most commonly, (3) if someone snapped a bracelet and managed to break it, the wearer had to perform the sexual act associated with that bracelet's color.[4]

Some commentators insisted that shag bands encouraged sexual misbehavior among the young; one referred to the sex-bracelet story as "one of the most dramatic media narratives about teen sex in recent years."[5] However, news coverage usually associated sex bracelets with younger preteens: in 2004, a Queens, New York, fifth grader attracted national attention when it was revealed she was buying bracelets for $1 and selling them to classmates for $1.25; five years later, Britain's *Sun* accompanied its story headlined "Bracelet Which Means Your Child Is Having SEX" with a picture of a mother and her eight-year-old daughter. Still, even the most fevered imaginations were likely to doubt that fisting had become a widespread practice on school playgrounds, and some commentators argued that shag bands were best understood as a contemporary legend, one of those supposedly true tales that spreads through the population.

However exaggerated, even ridiculous, the claims about sex bracelets might seem, the tale's spread was impressively wide. The story first gained wide currency in the United States in 2003, but by 2010, it could be found throughout the world—in England, Ireland, the Netherlands, Germany, and elsewhere in Europe and also in Brazil, Australia, South Korea, and other countries. Many people who heard and repeated the sex-bracelet story took it quite seriously and insisted that shag bands were a real, deeply troubling social problem.

Rainbow Parties

A similar concern, most often associated with junior high school students, involved *rainbow parties*. At these gatherings, each girl supposedly wore a different color of lipstick and then performed oral sex on each of the boys in succession, leaving rainbows of multicolored lipstick traces. The story was mentioned in a 2002 book, *Epidemic: How Teen Sex Is Killing Our Kids*, but did not come to widespread attention until an episode of *The Oprah Winfrey Show*, first broadcast in October 2003. Oprah asked her guest, journalist Michelle Burford, "Are rainbow parties pretty common?" and was told, "Among the 50 girls I talked to . . . this was pervasive."[6] In 2005, *Rainbow Party*, a novel aimed at young adults, inspired a good deal of critical commentary about the appropriateness of oral sex as a theme for adolescent fiction and about whether libraries should carry the book.[7]

The tale was linked to broader warnings about epidemic oral sex among teens that spread in the aftermath of the Monica Lewinsky scandal. Tom Wolfe, for instance, claimed in 2000 that junior high schools had a "new discipline problem": "Thirteen- and fourteen-year-old girls were getting down on their knees and fellating boys in corridors and stairwells during the two-minute break between classes."[8] Worries about *train parties*—"boys lined up on one side of the room, girls working their way down the row"—preceded the rainbow-party story, and commentators marveled that oral sex, once "considered to be an act even more intimate than that of intercourse," was now "largely seen as a safer, easier, less messy, and more impersonal precursor to or substitute for vaginal intercourse."[9]

In many ways, concerns about rainbow parties paralleled those about sex bracelets. In both cases, children or early adolescents were depicted as having more sexual knowledge than their counterparts in earlier generations had. Both sets of claims warned that young people's—and, in particular, girls'—sexual behaviors were governed by new customs (an obligation to engage in sexual acts when a bracelet was broken or to perform oral sex on all the boys at a rainbow party) that seemed to divorce sex from love and to foster promiscuity. Both concerns spread widely, even across international boundaries. And both led to debates, with skeptics dismissing the stories as false, highly unlikely, or at least exaggerated, as being merely contemporary legends.

Sexting

As the century's first decade wound to a close, there were news reports that high school students were *sexting* (using their cell phones to exchange sexual text messages and images). By June 2008, the Associated Press picked up the story with the headline "Teens Are Sending Nude Photos via Cell Phone."[10] In the digital age, what might be intended as a private communication (a partially nude self-portrait sent by a teen to her boyfriend) could become publicly available. In contrast to the sex-bracelet and rainbow-party stories, there was plenty of evidence that sexting really occurred. And sexting attracted extensive media attention, with reports from all across the country of teens (and even preteens) who had been caught sending sexual messages and the trouble they faced as a result. Parents were forced to respond, school administrators had to draft new policies, and law enforcement officials and legislators found themselves struggling with thorny questions: Was sexting a crime? Were these images child pornography? Did these adolescents need to be registered as sex offenders?

Although no one considered claims about sexting to be untrue, there were varied reactions to the story as it unfolded. Many people considered sexting to be very troubling behavior, another sign of kids going wild, and called for something to be done to stop teens from doing it, while others thought the matter was being blown out of proportion and found the proposals to curtail it excessive. Although there was debate over what to do about sexting, most agreed that it was a problem that needed attention. And it was not only adults in the U.S. who were worried about sexting; the issue made headlines in many other English-speaking countries as well.

While worries that children and youths were in danger from sexually exploitative adults had not vanished, the focus for public concern seemed to have shifted to worries that young people, especially girls, were sexually out of control. Even college-age young adults were not immune from scrutiny. There were warnings that *hooking up* was rampant on campus, posing threats of date rape, STDs, and other moral hazards. Although sex bracelets, rainbow parties, and sexting were not the only kids' activities that concerned adults, these issues received extraordinary attention in the media, even in legislative chambers, and they also became the subject of everyday conversations among ordinary people. There were debates: some people dismissed sex bracelets and rainbow parties as little more than rumors, figments of overactive adult imaginations, just as others argued that critics had exaggerated the dangers of sexting; but there were those who insisted that the threats were all too real and who called for action. This book explores how people handled claims that children and adolescents were engaged in troubling new sexual practices. While we will occasionally refer to hooking up and other issues, our focus will be on the three high-visibility concerns about younger kids: sex bracelets, rainbow parties, and sexting.

Concerns in Context

Concerns about sex bracelets, rainbow parties, and sexting followed a familiar pattern. In each case, claims that these were new forms of sexual behavior inspired a wave of commentary: journalists, cable-TV pundits, bloggers, and ordinary citizens repeated the claims ("Do you realize what kids today are doing?") and debated their significance (with responses ranging from "That's ridiculous!" to "Aw, we used to do the same thing when I was young" to "No! This is a disturbing new trend"). The way in which people reacted to these stories was likely influenced by a whole host of things: their own childhood experiences, their political leanings, and their exposure to related stories about kids and sex, just to name a few. In other words, concerns do not emerge in a vacuum. By understanding the cultural context in which these stories materialized, we can better explain the positions people took in response.

Concern over Sexual Play

Sexual play has historically been a subject of concern; after all, it is a common, although far from universal, activity during childhood and adolescence. It can be structured, as in the kissing games cataloged by folklorists. Thus, one 1959 analysis noted that preadolescents played "chasing kiss games," often on the playground: "In 'Freeze Tag' . . . you are permitted to kiss, and to chase, but only according to the rules." At junior high school gatherings, groups played "mixing kiss games" (e.g., "Post Office" or "Spin the Bottle"), in which "pairing occurs in the games but is characteristically of a momentary sort."[11] Older adolescents played "couple kiss games" that offer occasions for kissing (e.g., "Perdiddle" allowed a male who spotted a car with a missing headlight to kiss his date). Particularly at younger ages, kissing games seem to be largely about pursuit and poise, about exploring the boundaries of gender and daring to engage in a bit of intimacy.

One way to think about sex bracelets is in relation to the tradition of chasing kiss games: break the appropriate bracelet, and the wearer is obliged to hug or kiss. Claims that boys who break sex bracelets will be rewarded with sexual favors also resemble earlier, parallel tales about various sorts of "sex coupons" (e.g., intact labels peeled from beverage bottles, pull tabs from cans, etc.) that could be redeemed for sexual intimacy.[12] Similarly, stories about train parties and rainbow parties may seem less far-fetched because they suggest an escalation from earlier generations' parties featuring mixing kiss games. And this escalation to wilder sexual behavior fits into what many Americans seem to believe about how today's kids—especially girls—behave.

Of course, many adolescents engage in less structured sexual play —usually in couples, usually not including coitus—described in vague terms that shift over time. During the late nineteenth century, couples engaged in *spooning* or *canoodling*.[13] In the 1920s, the terms *petting*, *necking*, and *parking* (the term originally referred to couples stopping on the dance floor—parking—to kiss) became popular.[14] *Making out* seems to have emerged in the 1950s, *hooking up* even later.[15]

It is not as though there is anything new in worrying about youthful sexuality, although the concerns of earlier generations can seem quaint and amusing. For instance, during the 1920s, critics warned about *petting parties*. A front-page *New York Times* story ("Mothers Complain That Modern Girls 'Vamp' Their Sons at Petting Parties") quoted Janet Richards (a frequent commentator on social issues):

> The boys have gone to their mothers, said Miss Richards, and said: "Mother, it is so hard for me to be decent and live up to the standards you have set me, and to always keep in mind the loveliness and purity of girls. How can I do it with this cheek dancing, and if I pull away they call me a prude. And when I take a girl home in the way that you have told me is the proper fashion she is not satisfied and thinks I am slow."[16]

Similarly, the 1950s witnessed warnings about the new practice of *going steady*: "A popular advice book for teenage girls argued that going steady inevitably led to heavy necking and thus to guilt for the rest of their lives. Better to date lots of strangers, the author insisted, than end up necking with a steady boyfriend."[17]

Concerns about petting or going steady reflected worries about how social changes were affecting young people. As young people's access to first automobiles and then disposable income spread during the first six decades of the twentieth century, flirtation and courtship were less likely to occur under the supervision of adults. New forms of popular culture seemed to promote sexual awakening: movies allowed audiences to envision how romances might be carried out; new clothing styles—particularly the flappers' short skirts—revealed more flesh; and new music and dance styles seemed to promote sexuality. The troubled reactions to first jazz and then rock emphasized the primitive, sensual, uninhibited qualities of the new music.[18] In part, these reactions reflected concerns about racial contamination, worries that white youths might be corrupted by black music. But this new music also seemed sexy; commentators seemed fixated on its intense rhythms and moaning sounds.

Throughout the twentieth century, there was a growing sense that young people were living in a new world that operated according to new rules, that sexual play was more open, more common, and more extreme than in their parents' generations. Many people believed this was a slippery slope: movies put ideas into the heads of the young; fast music encouraged abandoning restraints; and, however innocent or playful petting might seem, it surely could lead to the loss of virginity, illegitimacy, and disgrace.

There is, then, a long line of commentators worrying about the sexual play of the young. Of course, what is considered shocking escalates with each generation: worries about close dancing become concerns about grinding, and anxieties about petting parties turn into stories about rainbow parties. Each generation's critics have managed to warn about a revolution in sexual manners, even as they often failed to acknowledge the longer history of concern about youthful sexual play. The point is that concerns about sex bracelets, rainbow parties, and sexting tap into longstanding worries about the extent and nature of young people's sexual activities today: believing that teen sex has become increasingly commonplace makes claims about organized oral-sex parties seem plausible.

Worrying about Kids

All three topics involved young people and sex, and the ways people responded to sex bracelets, rainbow parties, and sexting reflect a broader cultural context. Attitudes toward childhood and adolescent sexuality and sexual behavior fall into two broad camps. On the one hand, there are those who adopt what we might call a *pragmatic* stance. They argue that sexual curiosity and sexual expression are a fact of life, a normal, natural feature of childhood and adolescence, with which adults ought to make their peace. Freud's theories that emphasized sexual impulses as central to personality development in early childhood, like Kinsey's reports that presented data based on thousands of interviews with individuals about their sexual histories and showed that many people began behaving sexually during childhood, have influenced generations of thinkers who warned about the harms that might be caused by a sexually repressive upbringing. The pragmatic view encourages parents to view children's sexuality as normal, to deal with it calmly, and to avoid causing children to see sex as dirty, shameful, or disgusting. Overreacting to kids playing doctor or to masturbation threatens to do more harm than good. Of course, as teens mature, they run greater sexual risks—such as unplanned pregnancies or infections from sexually transmitted diseases—but the pragmatic position is that these risks should be addressed in ways that don't make things worse. People who accept this model advocate sex-education programs to help young people understand their own sexuality so that they can make wise decisions; they also campaign to make reproductive health services readily available to minors. The pragmatic camp's influence probably peaked in the early 1970s, when some children's-rights advocates called for lowering the age of consent and treating even early adolescents as capable of making responsible sexual decisions.[19]

By the late 1970s, a more traditional, *protective* approach was again attracting more support. Advocates of this position describe childhood sexuality in terms of threats to children. They warn about the dangers

posed by adult deviants—an array of abductors, pedophiles, child pornographers, sexual predators, date rapists, human traffickers, and others who might sexually exploit young people. In this view, children and
even adolescents are vulnerable innocents in constant danger of cor-
ruption, not only from predatory adults but from a popular culture that
exposes young people to sex. Rap music, R-rated movies, and especially
the Internet made it all too easy for children to be corrupted.[20] But the
protective critique has even broader recommendations. Sex education
—a centerpiece of pragmatic thinking—is seen as promoting sexual
behavior; if sex education has to be taught, advocates in the protective
camp insist that it should present abstinence before marriage as the only
truly safe sex. Similarly, protective critiques denounce the sexualization
of childhood; they claim that today's society forces children to "grow
up too fast" and that, in particular, childhood has become increasingly
sexualized.[21] In this view, today's children become aware of sexuality
and engage in sexual behavior at earlier ages than their counterparts in
earlier generations did, and this preternatural sexuality can be blamed,
in part, on suggestive toys, clothing styles, and other products being
marketed—particularly to little girls—that have corrupting effects.

Although much protective rhetoric emphasizes a need to revive traditional morality and is linked to conservative political and religious
positions, some feminists also adopt a protective stance. In their analysis, women and girls are the objects of male sexual exploitation rooted
in patriarchal male dominance, so that rape, pornography, and sexual
trafficking are all forms of gender oppression. When viewed through
the lens of gender, young people's sexual play can seem problematic,
and feminists—usually seen as political liberals—and conservatives
can find themselves allies in advocating a protective stance.[22]

Similarly, contemporary social scientists' treatments of adolescent
sexuality, the debates around it, and the policies that emerge from those
debates often focus on intersections of race, class, and gender.[23] However, as we noted in our preface, concerns over sex bracelets, rainbow
parties, and sexting have tended to depict these troubling activities as

involving middle-class, white kids—the targets of most protective concerns. Although commentators often worried that girls were especially vulnerable in these new sexual practices, race and class were rarely explicitly addressed by journalists.

The urgency of this pragmatic/protective debate over the best way to think about young people and sex reflected trends toward having fewer children and adopting more intensive parenting styles that raised the stakes for childrearing.[24] The debate had links to the broader culture wars that pitted more liberal advocates of greater sexual freedom against conservatives who invoked traditional moral values. Both positions coexist in contemporary America. There are occasional public debates, especially about the appropriate messages of public-school sex-education programs and about making contraception and abortion available to minors.[25] But most of the time, the advocates of each position talk mainly to those who agree with them. Still, each camp is out there, available to comment on claims that some new sexual behavior is making inroads among the young. As we will see, the debate between these two rival positions underpinned the ways people reacted to sex bracelets, rainbow parties, and sexting. But it is not enough to describe the ideologies that guided people. It is important to consider the broader cultural context within which these concerns emerged, the other sorts of issues that had been preoccupying people's attention.

Related Concerns

Discussions of social issues inevitably occur in a larger cultural context. What people have to say about a new issue is shaped by what they've heard recently about other topics. In particular, people tend to be quite interested both in children's well-being and in sexual matters. As a consequence, it is easy to draw lines between any new concern about kids and sex and other recent, related concerns. Of course, some issues fade from memory over time; most of us don't recall that petting or going steady once seemed controversial, but there are other, more recent topics that people are likely to recall and may consider relevant when they hear claims about sex bracelets, rainbow parties, or sexting.

POPULAR CULTURE AS A SOURCE OF CORRUPTION

There has been a long parade of commercial popular-cultural forms thought to have the power to damage innocent young people. Throughout U.S. history, reformers have denounced the corrupting influence of dolls, dime novels, nickelodeons, jazz, movies, comic books, television, blue jeans, rock music, miniskirts, video games, the Internet, and cell phones—to mention only a few of the media, styles, or popular-cultural products identified by moral authorities at different times as having had corrupting potential. Think of the controversial history of rock: there is a direct line of moral outrage about performers' personas—Little Richard of the '50s begat Alice Cooper of the '70s begat Madonna of the '80s begat Marilyn Manson of the '90s begat Lady Gaga; yesterday's threatening figure gradually evolves, first into a golden oldie and eventually into fondly recalled classic rock, even as commentators worry that today's performers are truly frightening.[26]

Concerns over sex bracelets obviously tapped into beliefs that commercial products themselves can be the source of dangerous contamination. Thus, a British MP insisted that parents "were 'absolutely horrified'" when they read the details on the [bracelets'] packaging."[27] Most school officials acknowledged that there was nothing inherently sexual about shag bands ("They're just bracelets"), but they argued that because many students knew the codes that assigned specific colors to different sexual meanings, the bracelets became sources of distraction. As a consequence, many schools banned the bracelets.

In contrast, the equipment needed to produce a rainbow party (lipstick) or sexting (cell phones with the capacity to send text messages and images) was ubiquitous and could hardly be banned. Still, commentators noted that the spread of cell phones in particular had created new dangers for young people. For example, after a sexting case in Massachusetts in which six junior high school boys were accused of sending a seminude photo of a 13-year-old girl, one journalist reported, "Parents, school administrators, and legal and technology professionals are reconsidering both the need for children to have cellular phones and the rules and laws that govern their use."[28]

THE PLAYGROUND AS AN ARENA FOR
TROUBLING BEHAVIOR

Probably all parents worry about their children's well-being, and sending children off to school, where they will be supervised by people outside the family, can be a source for concern (as evidenced by the rise of homeschooling as a way of circumventing whatever risks are thought to occur at school). In recent decades, the schoolyard playground has become problematized. There is a long tradition of folklorists appreciatively cataloging the games of children, even while acknowledging that kids' play can probe the boundaries of what can be said and done.[29] In contrast, some contemporary critics view the playground as a setting for bullying, aggressive behavior, social exclusion, and other troubling behavior.[30] In this view, the playground becomes a seedbed for bullying, sexism, racism, heterosexism, and violence. For instance, some feminists argued that sexual harassment at school is a common experience for girls, and they called on schools to institute tougher antiharassment policies. Such claims led to calls for closer supervision and efforts to regulate play, to discourage play that divides children by gender or that features play fighting. Some physical-education professionals promoted discouraging play fighting and banning dodgeball, tag, and other games thought to damage the self-esteem of children who lose, in favor of cooperative, noncompetitive games that foster solidarity.

Sex bracelets, in particular, could be criticized for introducing sexualized play into recess at a time when the playground was increasingly viewed as an arena for risky, harmful activities. At the same time, there were counterclaims that schools were overreacting to perceived threats, and reporters gleefully broke stories about elementary school children who fell afoul of zero-tolerance policies against bringing weapons to school (such as the Delaware first grader who was suspended for 45 days after he brought his Cub Scout spork—a combination spoon-fork utensil used for camping—to school to eat his lunch) or sexual harassment (various children have been disciplined for kissing a classmate, pinching, and so on).[31]

In short, adult attitudes about children's play—and especially sexual play—straddle an uncertain divide. On the one hand, people argue that curiosity, roughhousing, and the like are a normal, natural part of growing up, a way of learning necessary lessons. On the other, they worry that play is consequential, that it can harm children or lead them to develop in socially undesirable ways. But there is little agreement about how to distinguish between "good" and "bad" play.

Worries about the corrupting influence of popular culture or the dangers of the playground are merely examples of the ways the larger culture shapes social concerns. Reports that young people are wearing sex bracelets, participating in rainbow parties, or sexting one another emerge within a broader cultural context. They cannot be understood without appreciating how people are thinking and talking about other issues—including beliefs about the nature of childhood, the nature of childhood sexuality, the dangers that can threaten children, and the best ways of raising children. Our analysis will necessarily draw on this larger context in order to explain how and why these stories spread.

Characterizing These Stories

Our research on sex bracelets and rainbow parties indicates that people's reaction to these stories was mixed. Many believed that they really happened, while others were skeptical, claiming that they are just urban legends. Likewise, there was much variation in how commentators described the issues—some referring to them as arousing moral panic, for example. In this section, we discuss how we plan to characterize these stories and clarify what some of the terms we use mean.

Folklorists use the term *contemporary legend* (or, in popular speech, *urban legend* or *urban myth*) to describe stories that circulate largely through person-to-person contacts.[32] *Rumor* is legend's conceptual cousin; a rumor tends to be more localized, something said to have happened nearby and recently, although the precise boundary between rumor and legend is unclear. In the good old days, rumors and legends spread by one person talking to another face-to-face, but the communications revolution has meant that people pass along these stories in all sorts of ways, such as forwarding email messages or posting on Facebook. Contemporary legends usually have a moral; they suggest that the world is a dangerous place where gang members conduct lethal initiation rites, maniacs attack people at random, and other hazards await the unwary. These stories are usually told as true and are understood by both the person telling the tale and the person hearing it to be something that really happened. They often include some sort of authenticating evidence: the events supposedly happened at the local mall or to someone who knows someone that the person telling the tale knows. Yet these narratives can rarely be traced to a source that can be verified. In fact, a hallmark of a contemporary legend is the lack of specificity— or conflicting reports—regarding names, dates, and locations where the incident supposedly occurred.

We describe the sex-bracelet and rainbow-party stories as legends because they bear all the telltale signs just described. The problem with both terms—*legend* and *rumor*—is the widespread assumption that these stories are false, that they describe events that didn't happen, that never happened. In other words, when some people say that rainbow parties are just an urban legend, they mean that rainbow parties don't exist; similarly, other people may argue that if at least one rainbow party did occur, then the tale isn't just an urban legend. Both sets of claims are wrong. Contemporary legends exaggerate. Although we found no confirmed reports that either of these sexual games happened, it is impossible for anyone to prove that these activities *never* happened. The point is that even if some kids somewhere have put shag bands to sexual uses or participated in rainbow parties, at the very least there is no evidence that these forms of sexual play are at all common. In other words, it seems likely that far more people talked about these phenomena than ever engaged in the sexual acts described in the stories.

What makes a story a legend or a rumor is the way it spreads largely through informal means, as stories people tell one another; however, in our world, the media often pick up these stories and repeat them. Thus, reports passed through the schoolyard grapevine that sex bracelets have sexual meanings constitute a legend even though the story also received quite a bit of media coverage. Much of this book focuses on how these two stories—or legends—spread and how the media and ordinary people debated the meaning of these stories.

Sociologists would classify sexting—our third case—not as a legend but rather as a *social problem*.[33] This is another term that is often misunderstood. There is a commonsense assumption that a social problem is a social condition; that is, the social problem of sexting must refer to the people who may be harmed by sending or receiving sexual phone messages. A better way to think about social problems is to view them as a process, the way that people come to recognize something as troubling. A sociologist interested in understanding sexting as a social problem would ask who the people were who drew attention to the practice and named it and who argued that something needed to be done about it. When officials threaten young people with arrest and prosecution for sending sexual messages, when educators and legislators debate what sorts of policies or laws are needed to deal with sexting, and when the media cover all the things people are saying about sexting, they are part of that social-problems process.

No doubt far more young people sexted than ever engaged in any sex acts associated with sex-bracelet colors or had oral sex at a rainbow party, but it is not the actual amount of activity that makes the former a social problem and the latter two contemporary legends. Rather, it is the ways the two were discussed. Sexting received a lot of serious attention from adults who sought to devise formal policies to address the practice; it is that attention that makes it a social problem. In contrast, people may have talked a fair amount about sex bracelets and rainbow parties, but the focus of that talk was concern. There were no efforts to devise shag-band or rainbow-party laws and no concrete evidence that these sexual games were actually commonly occurring; they remained in the realm of legend.

Sex bracelets, rainbow parties, and sexting were all new concerns. Each quickly went from something that no one had ever heard of to activities that seemed ubiquitous. For a time, each attracted a fair amount of attention and debate. Sociologists sometimes describe such episodes, in which some new social issue becomes a subject of relatively sudden, relatively intense, relatively short-lived concern, as *moral panics* or, when the concerns involve sexual matters, *sex panics*.[34] Neither term is ideal, in that they both have misleading implications. The word *panic* evokes images of a crazed crowd stampeding to escape a burning building; it suggests irrational, highly emotional behavior. Describing the reactions to news of sex bracelets or sexting as panics seems excessive. Most of what we trace in this book is people *talking* about sex bracelets, rainbow parties, and sexting. Those discussions revealed that many people were *worried* about these phenomena, while others argued there was nothing to worry about and dismissed the issues. Still others, especially in the case of sexting, proposed taking action to try to stop young people from engaging in this behavior. Thus, we feel it is more accurate to describe people's reactions to these issues as indicative of worry or concern, not panic.

Lastly, we must address how we plan to talk about the young people who are at the center of these controversies. Although there was a tendency for people who worried about sex bracelets to claim that young, elementary-school-age children were using shag bands for sexual play, some people argued that the bracelets were used in high schools or even on college campuses. Similarly, there were disagreements about the ages of those who were supposedly participating in rainbow parties and sexting. There is no good, precise term to describe those who were believed to be engaging in these forms of sexual play. Constantly referring to *young people* or to *children and adolescents* seems stilted. Simply for the sake of variety, we will use those terms, as well as less formal ones, such as *kids* and *teens* more or less interchangeably, to refer to those younger members of society whose sexual play sometimes aroused concern.

Plan of the Book

Our central task, then, is to examine concerns about young people's sexuality in our new century. In particular, we are interested in how such concerns spread and how they are debated.

Chapter 2 examines how concerns—and particularly contemporary legends—spread across time and space. There are many studies of social problems that describe how activists, experts, and the mass media bring some new issue to the attention of policymakers. However, it has been more difficult to track the spread of more informal concerns, the stuff of rumor and legend. The Internet gives researchers new tools for understanding these processes, in that it allows us to locate more press coverage, such as articles in newspapers published in small communities, as well as claims by lots of amateur commentators who post statements on the web. This gives us a better sense of how concerns spread across time and space. Chapter 2 presents information about the diffusion of two contemporary legends: the stories about sex bracelets and rainbow parties.

Chapter 3 focuses on the role of television in spreading the sex-bracelet and rainbow-party legends. Because television is ubiquitous and often assumed to be an especially influential medium, its coverage merits special attention. TV journalists used a set of techniques to present sex bracelets and rainbow parties as disturbing, newsworthy trends. But TV coverage of these topics extended well beyond news programming, to talk shows and other forms of infotainment and even into the plot lines of a variety of TV dramas and comedies. Ultimately, we will argue that both sex bracelets and rainbow parties became cultural touchstones that no longer needed to be explained because they became so familiar to the public.

Chapter 4 shifts the focus to the ways ordinary people responded to these stories. Blogs, discussion threads, YouTube videos, and Facebook pages allow individuals to express their views. Online conversations about sex bracelets and rainbow parties were complex, filled with competing claims from believers (who found the stories credible and who worried about these new trends) and skeptics (who considered the tales implausible and dismissed them as insignificant). While most online comments on these topics were brief, when considered as a whole, they reveal patterns in the ways people respond to claims about kids gone wild.

Chapter 5 turns to the teen sexting crisis. An examination of the media's coverage of teen sexting reveals that unlike the sex-bracelet and rainbow-party tales, the phenomenon of teens sending and receiving sexual text messages and images via cell phones was well documented. However, the media's portrayal of sexting was still overblown. A closer look at sexting also illustrates how exaggerated claims about today's teens lead to more than simply heightened fear among parents and other adults—it can prompt efforts to control teens' behavior (in this case, to curb sexting). Ultimately, we will argue that exaggerated claims about teen sex distorts people's understanding, thereby unduly affecting people's decisions about how to respond.

Finally, chapter 6 concludes by asking why people buy into the hype about kids gone wild. We will look at how various groups, including teens, parents, school officials, the media, and advocates all have their own reasons for uncritically accepting stories about kids' sexual play. We will also consider how claims about "these kids today" lead to widespread beliefs about how young people behave sexually. Finally, we will contrast what "everybody knows" about kids and teens with scientific data on youth sexual behavior, which indicate that what people believe about the young is often wrong.

2

How Legends Spread

This is happening everywhere. It's happening in private
schools, it's happening in the suburbs, it's happening in the
cities. Kids are doing it everywhere.
—Stacy Kaiser, discussing rainbow parties on
The Doctors, 2010

Everyone realizes that concerns about social problems spread across
time and space. We find ourselves devoting attention to new worries—
fretting about subjects that have never before crossed our minds. Or
we hear that problems that once seemed far removed—restricted to
other countries or seemingly remote sectors of society—have migrated
and now loom closer to home. The concerns about sex bracelets, rainbow parties, and sexting illustrate such developments. All three topics
were unfamiliar when the new century began; each attracted considerable attention within just a few years. What happened? Answering this
question requires examining the dynamics of spreading concern and, in
particular, appreciating how contemporary legends travel in the Internet age.

In chapter 1, we characterized concerns about sex bracelets and rainbow parties as contemporary legends. For the most part, studying contemporary legends has been the job of folklorists, and they have been
particularly interested in the stories themselves. Folklorists tend to ask

such questions as, How does a particular story vary from one telling to another? or What sorts of elements or themes appear in different stories? When it comes to the truth of a particular legend, folklorists tend be agnostics; that is, so long as a story spreads primarily through informal means, they consider it a legend, regardless of whether it might be based on some actual event.

However, there was an important shift in the 1980s, when the idea of legends gained broader public attention. In 1981, Jan Harold Brunvand—a well-respected academic folklorist—published *The Vanishing Hitchhiker*, the first of a series of popular books about what he termed *urban legends*. Brunvand's books received a substantial boost from his frequent bookings on David Letterman's late-night talk show. Brunvand tended to characterize urban legends as false, so that his message could be understood as a form of debunking, telling readers and viewers, in effect, "You may have heard this story and believed it, but there's nothing to it; it's just an urban legend."[1]

The notion that urban legends were by, by definition, false spread widely. Journalists began dismissing stories as *urban legends* (or *urban myths*—a term that no folklorist would use).[2] The term diffused into popular culture: urban legends became the subject of dozens of popular books, as well as television series (such as *Big Urban Myth Show*, *Urban Legends*, and *Mythbusters*—which sometimes claimed to be testing urban legends), slasher movies (*Urban Legend*, *Urban Legends: Final Cut*, *Urban Legends: Bloody Mary*), board games (*Urban Legend*, *Urban Myth*), and even *Urban Legends and Shock Stories* trading cards. The Internet became a setting for various websites, such as Snopes.com, About.com: Urban Legends, and the Museum of Hoaxes, that devoted considerable attention to legends. Most of these books, TV shows, and websites treated urban legends as stories to be debunked: either something was true, or it was an urban legend. That is, people lost sight of folklorists' indifference to the truth of legends as the notion that *urban legend* was a synonym for *false* gained broad popularity.

The folklorists' conception of legends faces another challenge: confronting our heavily mediated world. Folklore as a field of scholarship traditionally focused on the spread of ideas—folk tales, folk songs, folk dances, folk crafts, and so on—through nonmediated channels. That is, folklorists viewed urban legends as stories that people told to one another, so that they were passed along by word of mouth. Of course, folklorists realized that sometimes a story might be repeated in the media, say, in a newspaper story or on a TV show, but they tended to dismiss the media's role as secondary, much less important than the informal, face-to-face channels by which these stories spread.

But the world was changing; people were communicating in new ways. Folklorists' research began recognizing that ordinary people could spread stories via photocopies, faxes, and email. The ability to attach documents and photographs to email messages created new possibilities for sharing jokes and stories. And the Internet created all manner of other opportunities to communicate—someone could create a website, a blog, or a Facebook page, post comments on others' sites, post YouTube videos, and so on—all of which provided ways to share legends.[3] Moreover, the Internet was an especially democratic forum. An individual might have his or her own website, but other websites were operated by major media organizations, as newspapers, magazines, television networks, and other traditional media struggled to adapt to a world that was increasingly communicating online. Whereas it once seemed possible to draw a clear line between information communicated via such mass media as newspapers or television and information acquired through informal conversations, that distinction has become increasingly blurred as both sorts of information spread online.

As we shall see, these developments have important consequences for how contemporary legends spread. Whereas the classic folklorists' conception of legend focused on stories spreading through informal, face-to-face contacts, our analyses of the dissemination of stories about rainbow parties and sex bracelets reveal a more complex pattern, in which the media play an important role in disseminating these stories. But first, we need to explain how we went about our research.

Studying the Dynamics of Contemporary Legends

The dissemination and transformation of rumors and contemporary legends are both self-evident and difficult to study. These stories travel; they spread both geographically across space and socially as they cross group boundaries. As they spread, they often change; for instance, the location where a killer waited for his victim becomes the local shopping mall, while tales about mistreated prisoners of war are updated to refer to a current conflict. Retelling alters elements in a story and produces what folklorists call variants or versions.[4] In some striking cases, key elements may shift as a story crosses group boundaries, so that blacks tell a tale in which whites victimize blacks, even as the version told by whites reverses the race of the victims and victimizers, or stories told in the U.S. about contaminated goods from Latin America and Asia are told in western Europe about North African imports, so that the versions told in different countries identify problems as coming from regions where their immigrants tend to originate. For example, tales of people bitten by poisonous insects lurking in bananas are told both in the U.S. (with the bananas reported to have originated in Central America) and in Europe (where the bananas are said to have come from Africa).[5]

Theorists have sought to explain these dynamics in various ways. Rumors have been classified, for example, as creeping (slowly spreading), impetuous (quickly spreading), and diving (recurring) rumors.[6] Oral transmission produces inaccuracies; even people trying to accurately repeat a message mishear or misspeak, so that a story morphs in transmission. Some modifications serve to make a story more relevant to the listeners; a tale about a crime at a local mall seems more compelling than one set far away. Further, a story's chances of being remembered and retold improve when it induces a significant emotional reaction; tales are likely to evolve in ways that make them more emotionally arousing.[7]

In the past, researchers found it difficult to study how rumors and legends spread and change. They might observe a particular story cropping up in diverse locations, and folklorists might collect and carefully catalog a few dozen variants, but efforts to trace stories back to their roots or to follow their spread across time and space seemed doomed to failure.[8] The transitory nature of rumor and legend, their dependence on oral transmission, and the modest media coverage they received (because the press had trouble finding people to verify these stories) made it difficult to track these stories.

The emergence of the Internet offers new resources for the study of rumor and legend.[9] The Internet collects and saves materials that would have been difficult, if not impossible, for earlier researchers to locate, including news stories from all sorts of media (e.g., smaller communities' newspapers), websites dedicated to unusual topics, and blogs and comments posted by a wide range of individuals. Moreover, databases and search engines provide tools for locating material on particular topics. These changes give us new tools for tracking legends across time and space.

Finding the Stories

Given the difficulties of randomly sampling Internet content, we sought to assemble a large, diverse body of sources that discussed sex bracelets and rainbow parties.[10] Our final sample contained more than 2,000 items related to sex bracelets and over 470 related to rainbow parties; these items ranged from newspaper and magazine articles focused on one of the topics to brief comments posted on a discussion thread linked to a website. While there can be no end to the number of hits elicited by web search engines, we continued collecting until we judged that we had achieved theoretical saturation (that is, additional hits did not lead to additional information).

We located comments in a wide range of traditional media, including books, pamphlets, magazines, newspapers, television (including news, entertainment programs, and talk shows), radio, and even a scholarly journal. However, the vast majority of the comments came from the

Internet via websites, blogs, comments on discussion threads, and Facebook postings. While professional commentators wrote a few online blogs, the vast majority of these comments came from ordinary people who were simply commenting about a topic of interest during a casual, online conversation, rather than participating in a formal research interview. These comments capture individuals exchanging views about sex bracelets or rainbow parties, in transmitting the tales and debating their meaning. While the anonymity of the Internet prevents us from authenticating the identities claimed in these comments, we note that people presented themselves as both youths and adults. Some dismissed the stories as having no basis in fact, while others insisted that these were real social problems.

On the one hand, it is as impossible to identify every mention of sex bracelets or rainbow parties as it is to track down every telling of any other rumor or contemporary legend. On the other hand, our sample represents a good-faith effort to be extensive and wide ranging: we searched a variety of databases, using several search terms. The fact that our various searches, although intended to cover different sorts of sources, produced a number of duplicate results suggests a level of thoroughness. More important, our results—spanning press coverage, books, and the Internet—reveal clear and consistent patterns with distinct waves of attention. In the case of sex bracelets, there were two waves: the first in 2003–4 and the second in 2009–10; in the case of rainbow parties, most attention was concentrated in 2004–5. The fact that these patterns are visible in all of our sources—both comments in the traditional media and the Internet discussions—gives us confidence in the validity of our findings.

Our sample tracks public commentary about sex bracelets and rainbow parties. Of course, these comments do not prove that young people who broke bracelets actually engaged in the sexual acts assigned to the bracelets' colors or participated in oral-sex parties. These stories must have been in circulation for some indeterminable time before they began to be reported on the web and in the press. We cannot know who first ascribed sexual meanings to the bracelets or who coined the term *rainbow party* or what was said. Still, given the suddenness with which these stories broke and the outrage and wide range of commentary they inspired, our inability to locate earlier sources suggests that the shag-band and rainbow-party tales may have been either relatively new or at least not especially widespread before they began attracting public attention. This means that these stories spread after the Internet was well established, so that we are able to track their diffusion across time and space in ways impossible for scholars studying earlier rumors and legends. And while our sample includes many reports by professional journalists, the vast majority of the comments in our sample come from ordinary people who posted comments on discussion threads or Facebook pages—individuals who identified themselves as parents, students, or simply concerned citizens. Thus, people often introduced themselves: "I am a mother and lil bit worried my 16 year old daughter is wearing these bracelets" or "PEOPLE!!!!! IM IN HIGH SCHOOL AND SHAG BANDS ARE JUST FOR FUN!"[11]

In sum, new electronic sources, including full-text databases and search engines, make it possible for us to track contemporary legends across time and space in ways previously impossible. We begin with the story about rainbow parties, which, we found, spread in a straightforward manner.

How Concern about Rainbow Parties Spread

The first time we could find the expression *rainbow party* being used was in a 2002 book, *Epidemic: How Teen Sex Is Killing Our Kids*, written by pediatrician Meg Meeker and published by a branch of Regnery, a longtime, leading conservative press. Meeker tells of treating a troubled 14-year-old patient who eventually described the event that had turned her life upside down:

She'd heard some kids were going to have a "rainbow party," but had no idea what that meant. Still, she thought it might be fun, and arranged to attend with a friend. After she arrived, several girls (all in the eighth grade) were given different shades of lipstick and told to perform oral sex on different boys to give them "rainbows." . . . Allyson was too stunned and frightened to do anything. When a girl gave her some lipstick, she refused at first but, with repeated pressure, finally gave in. . . . When it was over, she couldn't even look at the boy on whom she'd performed oral sex.[12]

Epidemic does not appear to have been particularly influential; the only attention it seems to have received were reviews on some conservative websites and mention in a couple of newspaper articles.

A year later, other media comments on rainbow parties reached vastly larger audiences. The August 2003 issue of *Seventeen* magazine contained "Oral Report" (an article on oral sex); the reporter quoted a Baltimore sex educator: "At one party I heard about, they played something called Make a Rainbow. The girls put on different colored lipsticks and took turns making a rainbow on all the boys' penises."[13] A couple of months later, the October 1, 2003, episode of *The Oprah Winfrey Show*, titled "Is Your Child Leading a Double Life?," included an interview with *O Magazine* writer Michelle Burford, who suggested that teens were involved in sexual practices that adults knew nothing about, including rainbow parties. Oprah asked, "Are rainbow parties pretty common?" and was told, "Among the 50 girls I talked to . . . this was pervasive."[14]

That *Oprah* episode in turn inspired the publication of *Rainbow Party*, a 2005 novel aimed at young adults. After hearing about rainbow parties on *Oprah*, an editor at a publishing house arranged for an author to write the book. It featured several junior high school students trying to decide whether they should attend a rainbow party; the female character who wants to host the party says she learned about them from a TV talk show. This novel inspired a good deal of outraged commentary, which served to further boost the visibility of rainbow parties.[15]

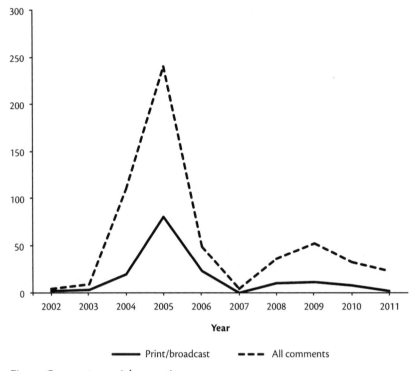

Fig. 2.1. Comments on rainbow parties, 2002–11

Figure 2.1 tracks the spread of comments about rainbow parties; the lower line shows comments in traditional media, including books, television programs, and newspaper and magazine articles; the upper line includes all comments, that is, those in traditional media plus various web-based comments. Note that the topic received next to no attention in 2002 and 2003 (the years when *Epidemic* and the *Seventeen* article were published and the *Oprah* episode was first broadcast). Interest in rainbow parties peaked in 2004 and 2005 (the year, remember, when the novel *Rainbow Party* was published); this was the period when Internet postings were most common. Next to the *Oprah* episode, the media comment that probably drew the largest audience was the March 2006 publication of Jodi Picoult's novel *The Tenth Circle* (which immediately entered the *New York Times* fiction bestseller list in second place).[16]

That novel involves a party where teens are "playing Rainbow," although this is largely extraneous to the plot, which hinges on a date rape that occurs after the party. Rainbow parties also were the subject of episodes on two cable-TV entertainment series—*Huff* (Showtime, November 2004) and *The Hard Times of RJ Berger* (MTV, July 2010). The great majority of the media comments came from the United States, although Canadian newspapers gave the story a good deal of attention in 2004 (when several pieces warned about "the Rainbow Club").[17] In contrast, there were only a couple of U.S. newspaper articles in our sample that appeared before 2005, when the press began covering the controversy surrounding the *Rainbow Party* novel. The story did travel to other English-speaking countries; there were several articles in the Australian press beginning in 2008 and one or two pieces each in New Zealand, England, and Ireland; but most of the media attention to the story was concentrated in North America.

Media reports that warned of rainbow parties insisted that their information came from young people. Recall that in *Epidemic*, Meeker stated that she'd first learned of rainbow parties from talking to a patient who had participated in one, just as the *Oprah* episode featured Burford saying that she'd spoken with 50 teens and that rainbow parties were "pervasive." In other cases, the source of the evidence was less clear: the sex educator quoted in *Seventeen* said she "heard about" a party. Similarly, Dr. Shannon Fox ("Sex Therapist/Mother of 3") in a momlogic video asks mothers, "Have your kids talked to you about rainbow parties? . . . It's starting in junior high, and they're very popular now. . . . [Oral sex is] happening on the school bus, it's happening in the bathrooms. I've had teenaged girls who've told me that they can't even go in the bathrooms at school because people are having oral sex in there."[18]

Yet our data do not reveal *any* popular comments about rainbow parties that preceded the media's coverage. The earliest web-based comments we were able to locate were definitions posted on the *Urban Dictionary*; the first two were posted on October 2, 2003 (the day after the

Oprah episode first aired), while a third was posted two days later and made it clear that the timing was no coincidence:

> *Rainbow party*: A word that was made up by Oprah in order to lure parents to be overly cautious for absolutely no reason.

> *Oprah: "Your daughter is a slut, she goes to rainbow parties, so lock her in a stone cell for the rest of her life, because I'm Oprah and I know everything!"*[19]

Much of the web-based commentary focused on the question of whether rainbow parties actually occurred, as we will discuss in more detail in chapter 4, or whether the tale was "just" an urban legend. But our data raise a different question: how much knowledge of rainbow parties was there prior to the media hyping the issue? Several media comments, including Meeker's *Epidemic*, the *Seventeen* article, and the *Oprah* episode, featured reports that some teens were talking about rainbow parties, but we have been unable to locate any informal commentary on the topic prior to it having received considerable media exposure. This suggests that the story may not have been in particularly wide circulation, that media coverage did a great deal to bring rainbow parties to broad attention, even raising awareness among the youth for whom the practice was supposedly "pervasive."

In other words, the folklorists' classic vision of legends traveling informally, by word of mouth, ignores the way stories spread in our more mediated world. It seems unlikely that Meeker and the journalists who reported in *Seventeen* and on *Oprah* conspired to arouse concern about a nonexistent threat; presumably all of them did hear something about teens having rainbow parties and passed along what they'd heard. That is, claims about rainbow parties probably were circulating among some young people. At the same, it seems telling that we cannot find any informal—that is, outside traditional media—mentions of rainbow parties until after the media's coverage began. This silence should not be attributed to some sort of prudish delicacy; folklorists have documented other fellatio-themed legends.[20] Rather, we might suspect that this was not a particularly widespread story or that it was just one of a set of tales about more or less organized oral-sex games, including train parties, chicken parties, stoneface, and so on.[21] With few exceptions, most accounts were second- or third-hand (for instance, the writer for *Seventeen* quoting a sex educator to the effect that she'd heard about one party where they'd played "Make a Rainbow"); these were stories about *other* kids doing shocking things.

It is easy to see why the notion of the rainbow party caught on and rival tales about train parties and such faded. The rainbow offers not just literally more colorful imagery but more dramatic elements. Having a rainbow party seemed to require more premeditation, organization, and coordination than other oral-sex events, making the tale all the more shocking. The various media accounts embellished the story in various ways: the fellatio might be public, with the boys sitting in a circle and the girls kneeling in front of them (as depicted in *The Hard Times of RJ Berger*), or it might be private, with a girl in a room, waiting for a boy to knock (as shown in *Huff*); some claimed that religious youth—intent on remaining virgins—were particularly at risk; others depicted it as a contest, in which the boy who acquired the most colors—or the girl who marked the most boys—was declared a winner.[22] Rainbow parties were criticized by conservatives on moral grounds and by people concerned with gender issues who viewed parties built around females pleasuring males as exploitative. It was a malleable story that could be told in lots of ways that could satisfy lots of different audiences. As early as 2005, brief allusions to rainbow parties as a telling example of the problems with contemporary culture began appearing in self-help books aimed at teens, guidebooks addressed to their parents, and more general works of social criticism.[23] Moreover, much of the media's treatment of rainbow parties actually focused on . . . the media's treatment of rainbow parties: Howard Stern complained that his program was sanctioned by the FCC for explicit content, while Oprah was free to talk about rainbow parties; and assorted commentators weighed in on whether publishers should be marketing *Rainbow*

Party and other relatively explicit young-adult novels and whether bookstores and libraries should make these titles available.

So the case of rainbow parties suggests that in our heavily mediated world, legends may originate among ordinary people, but they can spread much further and faster when they capture media attention. The online interpretations of rainbow parties by ordinary people— discussed in chapter 4—began well after the media had presented the story. It is impossible to divorce the informal commentary from traditional media coverage. Our second example, sex bracelets, reveals a similar, albeit rather more complicated, pattern.

How Concern about Sex Bracelets Spread

The earliest dated source in our sample of sex-bracelet comments comes from September 22, 2003: a definition for "shag band" posted on the *Urban Dictionary*: "The jist of em is if someone brakes your shagband u hav to shag em . . . thats about it really and they come in different colours n some mean different things ie.a kiss."[24] By the end of October, a newspaper in North Carolina and two in Florida ran stories reporting that local schools had banned the bracelets, and *Time* magazine printed a short piece that described the practice: "In a game some kids call Snap, they yank the rubbery bracelets from the wrists of fellow students to indicate which kind of sex they would like to have." Although *Time* acknowledged that "most kids seem to take the code as merely an inside joke," the article claimed that the practice had "spread internationally," noted that the bracelets had been banned in a Florida school, and quoted a 15-year-old from Los Angeles.[25] November 2003 featured televised broadcasts on NBC's *Today Show* and MSNBC's *Scarborough Country*, as well as on local news programs in Cleveland, Philadelphia, Washington, DC, and Dallas. In addition, the UPI wire service carried a story, and there were local newspaper articles in seven states (including pieces in the *Chicago Tribune* and the *St. Louis Post-Dispatch*); meanwhile online, Sex-bracelets.com offered "Your Complete Guide

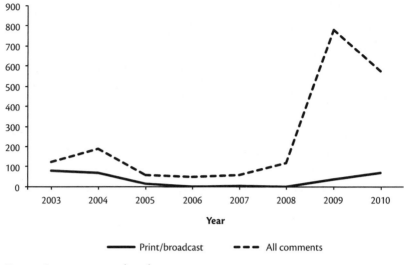

Fig. 2.2. Comments on sex bracelets, 2003–10

to Sex Bracelets," there was a warning posted at the *Education Coffee-house Newsletter*; and Snopes.com featured an email warning collected during November.[26] In other words, in just over two months, the sex-bracelet story had appeared on various websites, in four national print or electronic venues, and in local media in nine states and the District of Columbia.

Figure 2.2 shows the occurrence of shag-band comments by year, from 2003 to 2010. Again, the lower line includes only comments in traditional print and broadcast media (mentions in books, newspaper and magazine articles, and television and radio broadcasts).[27] The upper line includes all comments; these totals are much greater because they include online material from websites, discussion threads, and Facebook pages. While we were able to date all but about 25 of the 2,028 comments in our sample, we distinguish between traditional media and other comments because the traditional media can be assigned geographic locations, while it is frequently impossible to know for certain where people posting on the web are located.

Figure 2.2 reveals a clear pattern: both lines show two waves of interest in sex bracelets in 2003–4 and in 2009–10. Between 2005 and 2008, the subject attracted relatively little attention on the Internet and far less in traditional media. If we focus only on comments in traditional media (which allow us to identify their geographic origins), this wave pattern is reaffirmed. Figure 2.3 classifies each year's comments in traditional media by the nation where they appeared. Not only are the two waves more clearly visible, but it is apparent that there were localized waves in the traditional media's coverage. The shag-band story received concentrated attention in different countries in different years: in the United States during 2003–4, in Canada during 2004, in Australia (and also in the Netherlands—included in the graph's "Other" category) in 2009, in the United Kingdom in 2009–10, and in Ireland in 2010. The same wave pattern is apparent in figure 2.4, which examines the monthly number of comments in traditional media during the story's first year. Within the months when American attention was most intense, there were two distinct waves of attention—in November and December of 2003 and then again late in the following spring.[28]

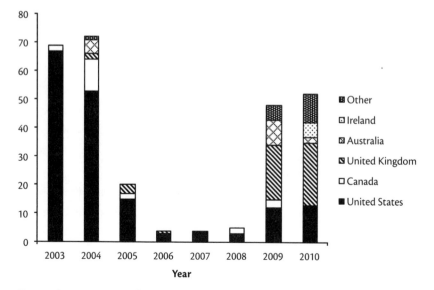

Fig. 2.3. Comments on sex bracelets in print/broadcast media, by nation, 2003–10

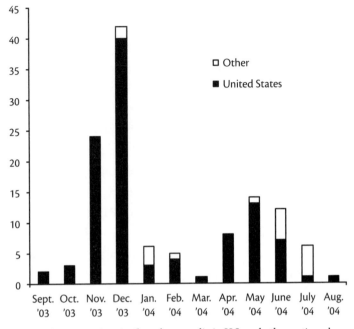

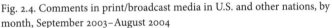

Fig. 2.4. Comments in print/broadcast media in U.S. and other nations, by month, September 2003–August 2004

On the one hand, these waves might simply reflect familiar media dynamics: a story that appears in a prominent news source, such as a wire-service report or an account in a major urban paper, might be picked up in local media. However, web-based comments during those same months also were concentrated in December and May, which suggests that popular interest in the story was roughly correlated with coverage in traditional media and, as in the case of rainbow parties, probably fostered by that coverage.

In short, our data reveal a pattern of relatively brief, localized waves of interest in shag bands. Far from dispersing steadily across time and space, the story moved in fits and starts—becoming established in North America in late 2003 and early 2004, then entering a period of abeyance, before reviving in the United States and Canada, while also spreading across the Atlantic and Pacific Oceans in 2009–10.

The Color Code

A substantial minority of the sources in our sex-bracelet sample sought to decode the meanings of shag-band colors by offering color keys. For instance, Internet vendors offered T-shirts and other items displaying "The Jelly Code" with five overlapping rings of yellow (labeled "Hug"), purple ("Kiss"), red ("Lap Dance"), blue ("Oral"), and black ("All the Way"). While it might be tempting to assume that these choices reflect some generally agreed on sense of the moral order of colors, the larger culture assigns most colors widely varying meanings—just think of all the different meanings assigned to red or blue.[29]

While some meanings for particular colors were relatively wide-spread, it was not uncommon to find alternative, contradictory color-coding schemes, even posted on the same website. Thus, while it might seem natural that "The Jelly Code" lets black—a color often associated with evil and deviance—represent what might be considered the most intimate (or dangerous) activity (sexual intercourse), people assigned other meanings to black. For instance, a discussion thread posted at the Jonesboro (Arkansas) Forum began with an August 31, 2008, message from "Concerned": "I heard teenagers are wearing sex bracelets and diffent color means something. My kid had a black one. can anyone tell me what all the colors mean???" Responses to this thread included,

According to Snopes.com Black means intercourse.

Black means they like it in the butt

Black: Has had sex, oral, anal, vaginal, multipule partner, same sex. Black is a catch all, but it could mean that you are attracted to the black race.

Black—indicates that the wearer will have regular "missionary" sex

It means you have had sex.

Black=it means sex in the dark

Black is with a condom

that means oral sex

well i can tell you that black is extream intorcourse[30]

In short, even within a single discussion thread organized in a small, middle-American city, commentators disagreed about a particular color's meaning.

Our large sample of comments about sex bracelets allowed us to search for patterns in the attributions of particular meanings to specific colors. Many comments gave keys—lists giving the meanings of various colors. We viewed the repeated use of a key as a variant of the shag-band tale; we identified 193 keys in total. Examining the similarities and differences in the meanings assigned to various colors allows us to identify patterns in the distribution and spread of variant versions of interpretations of shag bands.[31]

Table 2.1 identifies the ten colors most commonly mentioned in our sample of 191 color keys. Black was indeed the most commonly featured color—it appeared in 185 (i.e., 96%) of the keys—and there was a high level of agreement: 95% of the keys that mentioned black linked it to sexual intercourse.[32] But the table reveals considerable variation, both in the frequency with which colors were mentioned and in the degree of consensus about their meanings. Only about 79% of the keys included green, for instance, and less than half of those linked green to cunnilingus, with no fewer than 19 other meanings also assigned to that color. In addition to the ten colors listed in table 2.1 (all of which appeared in at least half the keys in our sample), we located keys that mentioned another 38 colors, each included in between 1 and 63 keys. In other words, there was considerable variation in which colors were mentioned and in the meanings assigned to each color.

This variety allows us to trace different combinations of meanings as variants of the shag-band story. Consider the key posted at Sex-bracelets.com (which dates back at least to November 2003).[33] That key attributes meanings to 14 different colors; in seven cases, it lists one or two alternate meanings (e.g., "Purple: anal sex [alternate meaning:

Table 2.1. Most Common Meanings Assigned to
Most Mentioned Sex-Bracelet Colors

Color	Number of keys*	Most common meaning	Percentage with most common
black	185	intercourse	95
blue	174	oral sex	87
yellow	169	hug	80
pink	166	hickey/love bite	53
purple	163	kiss	72
red	153	lap dance	82
green	152	cunnilingus	49
orange	146	kiss	64
clear	127	whatever	98
white	116	flash	78

* Total number of keys in sample = 193

holding hands, doggy style]"). Note that none of these three—markedly different—meanings ascribed to purple on this website became the most common meaning for purple (kiss) noted in table 2.1. If we examine the 193 color keys in our sample, we can find the Sex-bracelets.com key—same colors, same meanings—repeated four additional times, all during 2009–10. In other words, this key can be seen as a variant of the shag-band tale.

A more successful variant also was introduced in late 2003 at Amyth.com.[34] It listed meanings for 16 colors; according to this key, purple "indicates the wearer is willing to kiss a partner of either sex." This key was distinctive in that several meanings were phrased as indicating the bracelet wearer's *willingness* to engage in some sort of sexual behavior and in its use of capital letters and quotation marks. This particular variant proved to be especially popular; in many cases, the distinctive pattern of capitalization and punctuation was repeated, suggesting that individuals simply copied the key from one source and pasted it in their own comments. We found 33 keys belonging to this variant. In addition, two other variants with 3 and 10 keys closely resembled (i.e., had only a few meanings different from) the Amyth.com key, so that nearly a quarter of the keys belonged to one of these three variants.

We identified 18 distinct variants each containing between 2 and 33 keys; a total of 101 keys (52% of the keys in our sample) belonged to one of these variants. Some were short-lived, but others remained in circulation for years. Some seem to have been restricted to a single country, but others spread geographically.[35] Our analysis of the meanings attributed to different colors suggests the complexity and variability in legends. Whereas many keys differed from all others, other combinations of colors and meanings consolidated into distinct variants. Variants tended to increase as the legend spread and, even in an increasingly globalized world, distinct variants often emerged in particular countries. Like all references to shag bands, variants tended to be episodic, concentrated in particular places during brief periods.

What Makes a Legend

Comparing patterns of comments about rainbow parties and sex bracelets allows us to better describe how contemporary legends spread. We draw several lessons from our research. First, although folklorists focus on word-of-mouth transmission as the principal means by which legends travel, our evidence suggests that *today's media play a central role*. While it seems likely that the stories—that some kids had oral-sex parties featuring colored lipstick or that a broken gel bracelet might be a sex coupon—originated among the young, we located few informal comments made prior to the media repeating these tales. For both stories, media comments and informal comments tended to peak in the same years, even in the same months. Further, as chapter 4 demonstrates, media coverage inspired many of the informal comments, with people reacting in different ways, sometimes denouncing what the media said, sometimes endorsing it. It is impossible to know when or how most kids learned about sex bracelets and rainbow parties—did they first encounter these stories in the media, or did they hear them from a friend? But even if the latter is the case, what was the friend's source—another kid or a media report?

Second, attention to these topics tends to be *short-lived*. On the one hand, this should not surprise us. The media command our attention by reporting what is fresh or unfamiliar; that is why we call it *news*. News stories follow issue-attention cycles—a new topic is pointed out, and the more interesting or compelling stories inspire a wave of coverage until there seems to be nothing more to report, so that the topic seems to have become stale, old news, the audience becomes bored, and the media move on to new stories.[36] Similar dynamics shape legends; in order to spread, a legend must be interesting enough both to remember and to be considered worth repeating. But there are limits to how far even the best story can spread. When the response to "Hey, have you heard about . . . ?" becomes "Yeah, I heard that," stories lose their novelty, their appeal; they become familiar, no longer interesting. As a consequence, attention—both from the media and in the informal communications necessary for folklorists to consider a story a legend— is likely to spread quickly and then die off after a short time. Both the rainbow-party and the sex-bracelet stories display this episodic pattern.

Third, attention also tends to be *localized*. There is considerable evidence that legends travel from place to place; a story about, say, drug dealers peddling LSD-laced lick-on tattoos to preschoolers crops up in a city, then dies out, but is later spotted in another city. Our data reveal localized patterns of media coverage in different nations. We can trace the spread of stories about rainbow parties and shag bands from one country to another. These stories received short-lived media attention, but different countries' media covered these stories at different times. Often, a newsworthy event (such as the publication of a young-adult novel about an oral-sex party or a news story about a fifth grader selling sex bracelets to her classmates) or attention in a prominent media venue (such as *Time* magazine or *Oprah*) led to a cluster of media reports within just a few weeks.

Fourth, the key difference between a contemporary legend and social issues is that *social issues receive vastly more attention* than legends. This chapter's analysis of the spread of rainbow parties and sex

Table 2.2. Numbers of Articles about Rainbow Parties,
Sex Bracelets, and Sexting in Various Literatures, 2003–12

Type of literature	Rainbow parties	Sex bracelets	Sexting
Newspaper articles[a]	18	30	3,095
Years	2003–9	2003–10	2008–12
Law review articles[b]	3	0	235
Years	2006–8	—	2009–12
Medical articles[c]	0	0	18
Years	—	—	2009–12
Education articles[d]	0	0	20
Years	—	—	2009–12
Criminal justice articles[e]	0	0	27
Years	—	—	2009–12

[a] ProQuest Newspapers database
[b] Lexis-Nexis Law Reviews database
[c] MEDLINE database
[d] ERIC database
[e] Criminal Justice Abstracts database

bracelets has made the point that media attention played a key role in this process. We have been highlighting the media's importance, precisely because folklorists tend to downplay the media's role, so our argument claims that these legends received more media attention than might be expected. But how much is more? Table 2.2 helps put matters into perspective. It compares the amounts of coverage the media gave each of the legends and to sexting. The table's top line looks at the number of newspaper articles on each topic indexed in the ProQuest Newspapers database. It is instantly apparent that sexting received roughly 100 times more attention than either of our two legends. If anything, this comparison understates the magnitude of the difference, because the newspaper articles about sexting were concentrated in the four-year period 2009–2012.[37]

In addition, table 2.2 presents data from databases that index the literatures in four different professions: law, medicine, education, and criminal justice. We might expect this coverage to lag behind newspaper reports a bit. After all, newspapers depend on their ability to report events soon after they occur, but it takes more time to assemble the necessary data, write an article, and get it accepted by and published in a law review or a professional journal. Still, all four literatures reveal a good deal of attention to sexting in the three years 2009–2012. Moreover, the difference between sexting and the two contemporary legends could not to be clearer. Although media reports sometimes noted that many schools were banning sex bracelets and that physicians were concerned about the health risks of oral sex, there were *no* medical articles, *no* articles in the literature aimed at educators, *nor any* articles in the criminal justice literature regarding either legend. The table does note that three law review articles mentioned rainbow parties, but these were all passing allusions. In contrast, many of the 235 law review articles about sexting actually focused on sexting and bore titles such as "The Teen Sexting Dilemma" and "Sixteen, Sexting, and a Sex Offender."[38]

These data reveal the difference between contemporary legends and social issues. Legends are basically stories that get repeated, often through informal channels but increasingly—in our contemporary society—via the media. Some of these stories travel great distances and find their way into news reports, online discussion threads, popular culture, and so on, but although they remain entertaining—perhaps surprising, troubling, shocking—stories, they don't inspire much institutional reaction. Social issues may also be illustrated with stories—in the case of sexting, there were reports of young people sending each other sexually charged messages on their cell phones—but those stories receive much more media attention than legends. In addition, reports about social issues inspire reactions in serious institutions, such as law, medicine, and education. Some people may have worried about rainbow parties and sex bracelets, even insisted that they were widespread, but there were also skeptics who considered these tales implausible. In contrast, state legislators, law enforcement agencies, and schools and school districts viewed sexting as something that was certainly happening, that seemed to be relatively common, and that, under current policies, could even lead to tragic consequences, such as felony arrests on child pornography charges, formal designation as a sex offender, or even a teen's suicide. Thus, a policy debate emerged, as people in positions of authority considered how this social issue should be resolved. The result was that sexting received far more coverage in conventional news channels and also in assorted professional literatures.

This chapter has examined the spread of two contemporary legends. Our analysis suggests that folklorists conceive legends too narrowly, as stories that travel by word of mouth, barely affected by their occasional coverage in the media. In contrast, we have argued that stories of rainbow parties and sex bracelets involved a more intensive interaction between ordinary individuals and the media: those who reported these stories in the media claimed to have heard them first from ordinary young people, but their coverage in turn spread knowledge of these sexual practices to a wide audience, so that most informal comments depended on the media first disseminating these tales. We have also shown that attention to these stories is relatively short-lived and that it tends to be localized. And we also argued that there are limits to media coverage of legends, that rainbow parties and sex bracelets attracted far less attention than did sexting, which became a much more heavily covered social issue, debated by policymakers.

While this chapter has focused on the ways legends spread, the next two chapters look more closely at how these stories are told, both in the media (as represented by the television coverage of rainbow parties and sex bracelets examined in chapter 3) and in the informal online discourse of ordinary people (the subject of chapter 4).

3

Parents Beware

Packaging Legends as TV News

We're going to turn now to a disturbing new trend in the
news among young girls. Very young girls. It has to do with
jelly bracelets. And you've seen them. . . . We want you to
hear now the kind of thing that is going on. And we want to
warn you if you want to have your own kids leave the room
because you're going to hear from 11 year-old Megan. . . .
And remember, she's in the fifth grade.
—Diane Sawyer, on *Good Morning America*, 2004

While newspaper stories, magazine articles, local TV news broadcasts, and other media reports ran stories about rainbow parties and
sex bracelets, nationally broadcast television programs probably had
the greatest effect on the public's awareness of these tales. Television
reaches large audiences. On a typical day, a program on a cable news
network, such as MSNBC's *Scarborough Country*, might have about
300,000 viewers, while the broadcast networks' morning shows, such
as NBC's *Today Show*, reach as many as five million viewers. These programs feature well-known, trusted media personalities, such as Diane
Sawyer, who may have been able to persuade their audiences that the
stories were true or at least interesting enough to repeat during their
next watercooler conversation.

As discussed, media attention to rainbow parties and sex bracelets occurred in short-lived waves. Coverage on television news programs—including the shows on cable news channels and the major networks' morning programs—tended to be concentrated during these waves. National television news coverage tended to follow some bit of breaking news, such as a report of a school banning jelly bracelets or the release of the novel *Rainbow Party*. But other television shows occurred outside waves of coverage; for instance, a talk-show program about some larger topic, such as teen sex, might make reference to shag bands or rainbow parties. TV dramas might also allude to these tales, but the lead time required to produce episodes of these shows meant that their broadcasts rarely coincided with news coverage.

Regardless of the network or the type of show, television tended to depict sex bracelets and rainbow parties in fairly consistent ways. TV coverage tended to be both credulous, in that it rarely cast doubt on these stories, and alarming, in that it portrayed kids' sexual play as troubling threats to young people. This chapter explores the techniques adopted when TV tried to convince viewers that sex bracelets and rainbow parties were disturbing, newsworthy trends. These techniques reflected the formulas used to produce TV shows, so we begin by discussing television's formulaic content.

Formulas as Framework for Covering Contemporary Legends

Most popular culture is organized into genres, that is, a familiar story format. Popular novels can be classified as romances, thrillers, science fiction, and so on, just as popular music can be divided into country, rock, and hip-hop. Each genre has a formula, a set of conventions: readers expect that a romance will end with the heroine finding true love or that the detective will solve the murder mystery. Genres have their fans (who enjoy a formula's familiar contours) and their detractors (who often complain about the formula's predictability).[1]

Television, of course, has its genres (such as dramas, talk shows, and news programs), and these genres have their own formulas. Anyone who watches more than a couple of episodes of a TV show learns to spot the recurring elements: *X* tends to occur at point *Y* in each show and is treated in way *Z*. Virtually all TV programs—including news shows, talk shows, and other forms of nonfiction programming—display this sort of regularity. The content may vary from one episode to the next—after all, we expect each day's news to be different from every other day's—but that content is presented within a framework of conventions.[2]

We might imagine that covering contemporary legends offers challenges to TV programs. After all, while some people may firmly believe in the truth of a particular contemporary legend, the evidence to support these tales is fairly thin. Therefore, TV might frame these as controversial topics and present them as debates between people warning about the dangers of sex bracelets and rainbow parties and those skeptics who challenge the believers' claims (as chapter 4 demonstrates, some online forums hosted such dialogues). Although some TV programs feature debate as a formula (think of those political shows where liberals and conservatives rail against one another), the coverage of shag bands and rainbow parties rarely cast doubt on these stories. A different set of conventions was at work.

You Better Listen Up: Sensationalistic Story Introductions

In order to attract viewers, television news and newsmagazine programs typically introduce stories with *teasers* meant to keep viewers tuned to the program. This tactic not only maximizes the chances that viewers will keep watching but sets the stage for the story. The introductions to coverage of sex bracelets and rainbow parties typically warned viewers about this dangerous new trend. These teasers often targeted parents and presented sex bracelets or rainbow parties as something they ought to know about, so they could prevent their children from participating in practices that threatened young kids, not somewhere but everywhere.

The first national television program to cover sex bracelets was MSNBC's *Scarborough Country* (broadcast during prime time on November 13, 2003), which adopted a tone designed to sensationalize the story and generate fear among the public, especially parents. Joe Scarborough, the program's host, began,

> Kids gone wild, children out of control, experimenting with sex before they reach their teens, using drugs and going on violent rampages in schools. . . . What should concerned parents do? . . . Now, as some of you may or may not know, one of the latest fads going around our kids' schools are jelly bracelets. What you might think is good, clean fun could be ruining your children's lives. Some kids call them sex bracelets.[3]

The very next day, on the top-rated morning program, *The Today Show*, cohost Matt Lauer introduced a report on shag bands: "Well, parents beware. Your teenage daughter's favorite accessory may be a kind of sexual code. NBC's Don Teague reports on the way schools are now responding to the many colors of the rubbery bracelets called jellys."[4]

Although coverage of sex bracelets continued in print media and on the Internet, sex bracelets faded from national TV coverage for six months, presumably because the story did not offer a new angle that could keep it fresh. Then, in May 2004, programs on three networks discussed the topic on three consecutive days. This coverage followed a *New York Post* story about a fifth grader who had been expelled from her school for selling jelly bracelets to fellow students; all three programs featured interviews with both the student and her mother. On May 24, *The Big Story with John Gibson* on Fox News kicked off this wave of coverage with this sensationalistic introduction: "OK, parents. Heads up. Kids today may be trading sex acts like we traded baseball cards. Stuff we didn't even know about back then is literally a game to some young people today. Heather Nauert has more now on something called 'sex bracelets.'"[5] *Scarborough Country* followed the next day, this time emphasizing not the gender-neutral "kids gone wild" angle but warning parents about their middle-school-age daughters: "Have you noticed your daughter wearing colored jelly bracelets? Well, if so, they could be sex bracelets. We're going to tell you about the latest trend that is sweeping middle schools, with an 11-year-old girl who was expelled for wearing them."[6] The following day, Diane Sawyer of *Good Morning America* picked up the topic (the teaser for its coverage is at the beginning of this chapter)—notably warning parents to have young children leave the room yet quickly noting that the featured speaker was an 11-year-old fifth grader.[7]

Lead-ins to coverage of rainbow parties followed the same pattern. For instance, Miles O'Brien, the host of CNN's *American Morning* began, "Do you know what a rainbow party is? If you're parents, you better listen up. Your teenage daughter might know. She's reading about it in a sexually explicit young-adult novel that puts an emphasis on 'adult' to say the least."[8] Similarly, MSNBC's *The Situation with Tucker Carlson* covered the purported oral-sex craze among middle schoolers, in a story that referenced rainbow parties. "Thirteen-year-old girls having oral sex? Everybody knows it happens. But according to a number of recent press accounts, it happens a lot. Not just in bad neighborhoods but in your neighborhood. Probably in your child's school. Scared yet? If not, you don't have a 13-year-old daughter."[9]

The language used by news programs to introduce the topics they cover on any given day is strategically chosen. It is meant to grab the viewers' attention by using scare tactics and to keep them tuned to the show. The story introductions we analyzed, whether the segment was about rainbow parties or sex bracelets, (a) emphasized the involvement of young kids, especially girls, (b) warned parents that they were ignorant of what their own children were doing in secret, and (c) declared the phenomenon to be widespread. Often, the introductions made it clear that wearing sex bracelets and going to rainbow parties were going on among the kids who "matter" to the largest share of the viewing audience: white, middle-class kids. This formula was standard; the words adopted by different programs were almost identical.

By sensationalizing their lead-ins to these stories, the news programs successfully gave the impression that sex bracelets and rainbow parties were important topics that should be taken seriously.

Just the Facts

In order for national television programs to justify their sensationalistic, sexually suggestive coverage, they presented the sex-bracelet and rainbow-party stories as factual, in spite of very weak evidence that either was actually happening. In contrast, newspaper articles were much more likely to suggest that the stories might be contemporary legends. For example, when the Associated Press ran a December 2003 story about sex bracelets, it quoted the vice president of Teenage Research Unlimited, a firm that tracks youth trends: "No one could point a finger to anyone who was actually doing [the sex-bracelet game]."[10] Similarly, a January 2004 *Washington Post* story argued that sex bracelets were likely an urban legend, while a 2005 piece in the *New York Times* titled "Are These Parties for Real?" asked whether rainbow parties were an urban legend:

> "This 'phenomenon' has all the classic hallmarks of a moral panic," said Dr. Deborah Tolman, director of the Center for Research on Gender and Sexuality at San Francisco State University. "One day we have never heard of rainbow parties and then suddenly they are everywhere, feeding on adults' fears that morally bankrupt sexuality among younger teens is rampant, despite any actual evidence, as well as evidence to the contrary."[11]

Yet when national television programs covered these stories, most presented the sexual games as fact and scarcely mentioned that some authorities considered these tales to be urban legends. They also offered so many details and specifics about the stories that many viewers may have concluded they "must be true."

For sex bracelets, one detail the television media focused on was which sex act each colored bracelet symbolized. The color codes varied somewhat from program to program, and there were also titillating references to colors representing something so risqué that the host could not even share the true meaning. According to the initial *Scarborough Country* coverage of sex bracelets, "The kids say they have a sexual meaning. The yellow ones mean hugging, purple ones kissing, a red one means a girl will give a lap dance. A blue one means she will perform oral sex. And a black one means she will go all the way."[12] Six months later, the same program embellished the color code, in the process significantly altering the supposed meaning of purple: "A black bracelet means sexual intercourse. Blue is for oral sex. Red is lap dance or French kiss. White is for homosexual kiss. Green means you're going to have sex outside. And if you got a light-green glow-in-the-dark, that means using sex toys. Brown, purple, and silver represent acts that shouldn't be mentioned on a family program like *Scarborough Country*."[13]

In addition to informing parents and other viewers about the color codes, the television hosts also presented the sex-bracelet story as if there was no doubt that this was a widespread problem. They did this by identifying specific locations where it was happening and ultimately claiming that the game was "everywhere."

We hear stories every week. And there was one in Dallas this past week of an eighth-grade girl having sex with a tenth-grade boy. And we hear these stories every week. (*Scarborough Country*, November 13, 2003)

The controversy isn't just limited to Florida. Schools around the country are now beginning to ban these jelly bracelets, and some students are now fighting back. (*The Today Show*, November 14, 2003)

This is something that we've been hearing that kids have been wearing throughout the country, in California, in Georgia. What do you think when you hear that these bracelets are being worn pretty much everywhere? (*The Big Story with John Gibson*, May 24, 2004)

And again, it's not just one case in New York. Again, it's around country. It's Pennsylvania. It's in South Carolina. I come from a very conservative area, and I've heard horror stories about what goes on in middle schools there. (*Scarborough Country*, May 25, 2004)

Talk-show host Montel Williams went further and warned his viewers that sex bracelets were not just a problem in the U.S. but "all over the world."[14]

The coverage of rainbow parties included graphic descriptions of the practice. On *Oprah*'s episode about the secret life of teens, journalist Michelle Burford explained, "A rainbow party is an oral-sex party. It's a gathering where oral sex is performed. And a rainbow comes from all of the girls put on lipstick and each one puts her mouth around the penis of the gentleman or gentlemen who are there to receive favors and makes a mark in a different place on the penis—hence, the term *rainbow*."[15] Similarly, a therapist guest on the syndicated medical talk show *The Doctors* insisted that rainbow parties were happening "everywhere."[16]

In national television's accounts, sex bracelets and rainbow parties were presented as true stories. In spite of the questions raised in widely circulated newspapers and other media, TV insisted there had been many incidents of kids participating in these games, enough cases to justify describing them as nationwide trends. By describing the games' specifics and providing locations where they took place, the shows lent credence to the stories. This coverage left viewers little room for doubt.

Sources

In order for TV-show hosts to back up the claims they were making, they often turned to guests who could provide firsthand accounts or further knowledge about teens' sexual play. In coverage of sex bracelets, guests would appear on camera to recount what they knew about the illicit game. Students, parents, and school officials were among those giving on-camera interviews. One cannot help but notice that almost all the kids interviewed were girls. Presumably, the notion that very young girls were willing participants in illicit sex games made the coverage more frightening to parents; if girls, the ones traditionally held responsible for limiting sexual intimacy, were no longer setting limits on sexual play, anything might happen. Although television producers had no trouble finding people to talk about shag bands, including girls and their mothers, a careful reading of the transcripts showed that no student admitted actually playing the game, and no parent or school official could identify a concrete case of it happening. However, this fact did not deter these guests from joining in the chorus warning the public that the sex-bracelet game was indeed widespread.

In several interviews, kids confirmed that the bracelets had sexual meaning, but they would be sure to point out that they did not act on those meanings. On *The Today Show*, an eighth-grade girl from a school in Ohio said, "I heard they have sexual meanings, but I don't pay attention to those meanings."[17] The same fifth-grade girl—Megan—appeared on three shows; her connection to jelly bracelets had made the news, both print and television, after she was expelled from a Catholic elementary school in Queens, New York, for selling the bracelets to classmates. Yet, like other kids who were used as sources for the story, Megan stated that she had never engaged in sexual acts due to the bracelets:

JOE SCARBOROUGH: You know, Megan, this obviously would shock a lot of parents across the country, that these bracelets are being used to send —what is it, to send the message out to boys of what you will or what you won't do [sexually]?

MEGAN: I don't do that stuff. I just collect the colors. Mostly, I have all the colors except orange. I just collect them. I don't do any stuff like that.[18]

In spite of the kids' denials, savvy television hosts made every effort to turn their child sources into eyewitnesses to grade school debauchery.

DIANE SAWYER: Now, Megan had talked about the fact that it—and again, [parents], if you want to have your kids leave the room—that [the colors do] mean oral sex or . . . lap dancing. And that's what girls are expected to do. She also told us what she sees her fifth-grade friends doing.

MEGAN: Sixth graders in my, in my school, some . . . some of them were . . . were kind of like doing the French kiss and stuff. But they weren't doing like . . . like the [other] stuff. All . . . all they did was the French kiss.

SAWYER: So they were *starting with* the French kiss in her school. That's what she had actually seen.[19]

Given the young age of the kids who served as sources for this story, they often appeared on camera with a parent by their side. The parent would serve as a secondary source of information on sex bracelets. Although none of the girls interviewed admitted actually doing anything sexual, the parents who appeared warned that the game is a clear indicator that kids today are becoming sexual too soon and something must be done to stop it.

MOTHER: It's shocking. You know, they're middle school kids. When I was in middle school, I never thought about anything like that.[20]

MEGAN'S MOTHER: I am outraged, and I'm, like, terrified. . . . I hope that the parents and grandparents who are out there listening . . . they should ban [jelly bracelets] from their—all places like 99-cent stores. They should not sell them to children.[21]

In addition to calling for a ban on jelly bracelets, the same mother, while appearing on *Scarborough Country* the next day, echoed other parents' sentiments that it was not like this when she was a kid.

MEGAN'S MOTHER: I'm horrified as a mother. I grew up in the '80s, and . . . I played with Barbie dolls back then. But this, when I heard this, me and my husband were just shocked and outraged. It's like, wow. I taught [my daughter] about the birds and bees, but this is too much. I'm sorry.[22]

In a couple of cases, school officials were used as sources to lend credibility to the story. Although no school official could confirm a case of the sex-bracelet game actually happening, these officials still expressed their concerns as if it was a real phenomenon. A school board member on *The Today Show* insisted, "Kids in the fifth, sixth, and seventh grade should not be talking about lap dancing or oral sex or even concerned with that."[23] Similarly, a *Dr. Phil* episode about the sex-bracelet controversy included a school board member and a parent who debated whether their school should ban the bracelets. Neither guest could confirm that the game was being played, only that some kids wore the bracelets.

> SCHOOL BOARD MEMBER: My son right now is in the fifth grade. . . . I happen to know that there was one child in his class who wore the bracelets. I'm absolutely appalled, and I'm devastated that it's the age of the children that are discussing it, that we have 9- and 10- and 11-year-old kids. How awful is it, as adults, that we've allowed to erode to the fact that lap dancing is something that's cool in middle school? And I'm—that just makes me sick.[24]

Like parents, school representatives also claimed that kids' sexual behavior was more out of control than in previous generations. On *The Montel Williams Show*, the host prompted a veteran high school teacher in the audience:

> WILLIAMS: Twenty-two years you've been sitting in classrooms. Now, tell me, do you think the kids of today are more sexually active and sexually charged than the kids of, let's say, five years ago?
> TEACHER: I do.

WILLIAMS: And so should parents be alarmed right now? Because I don't
know if parents really understand what is going on in schools. They
don't know that there's this little bracelet thing happening.[25]

As this exchange illustrates, the most compelling source of information
on sex bracelets often was not one of the guests but the television host.
If a student, parent, school official, or other expert did not say enough
to convince the audience that sex bracelets were something they should
worry about, the host was always there to make sure viewers did worry.
Consider this exchange between Montel Williams and another audience member:

WILLIAMS: You got any kids at home?
MOTHER: Yes. My son just turned 14, and my daughter's 9.
WILLIAMS: Really? Now, your 14-year-old son, did he tell you about the
    [sex] bracelet?
MOTHER: I've never heard anything about any bracelet.
WILLIAMS: Really?
MOTHER: I don't think they have those in Florida.
WILLIAMS: That's a lie![26]

Similarly, on a segment of CNN's *American Morning* about the release of the novel *Rainbow Party*, host Carol Costello and her guest had
an exchange in which Costello continued to press:

COSTELLO: So what's a parent to do? Atoosa Rubenstein, editor in chief of
    Seventeen magazine, joins us to talk about the book and the contro-
    versy surrounding it. . . . Frankly, this book shocked me. . . . Do teen-
    agers really buy into this stuff?
RUBENSTEIN: I have to tell you . . . I've been doing this for a long time. I
    have never heard of a girl who's actually attended a rainbow party.
COSTELLO: But the idea of a rainbow party does go through teenage circles?
RUBENSTEIN: I think that it's more about the titillation of books like the

one that we're talking about. You know, it's more of a fantasy. . . . But it doesn't mean it's what they're actually participating in. . . . I mean, I have to tell you, the numbers prove that girls today are actually starting to go toward modesty in their own lives. The number of virgins is up. Fifty-three percent of teens are virgins. The pregnancy rates are down. So there's a lot of good news. But I do think that steamy, sexy headlines like this are what get parents' attention and ratings and viewers and—

COSTELLO: You know, I don't know though. Did you watch the Oprah show where she talked about oral sex among teenagers and how teenagers really don't consider that sex? I mean, where do they get that? Is it Britney Spears and Lindsay Lohan?[27]

Often, then, the host proved to be the most important source for the story. The format for these programs allowed the hosts to shape the conversation and offer their opinions on the topics being covered. In fact, several hosts indicated that they personally believed that sex bracelets or rainbow parties were major problems. For example, on Fox's *Hannity & Colmes* program, cohost Sean Hannity started off his discussion with his guest, sex therapist Judy Kuriansky, by declaring that he believed rainbow parties are real.

HANNITY: This is happening.

KURIANSKY: Yes. And, you know, it isn't just that the girls are wearing different color lipsticks. They're doing something.

HANNITY: They're performing oral sex on these boys, and the idea is for the boys to have all the different color lipsticks.

KURIANSKY: Yes, as rings on their private part.[28]

Likewise, the hosts of *The Doctors* affirmed the dangers of rainbow parties after a guest, psychotherapist Stacy Kaiser, described them:

KAISER: Well, back in the day, like five years ago, you were hearing about parties where people played Spin the Bottle and Truth or Dare, and now it's escalated to a whole other level. The big thing I'm hearing about now is called rainbow parties, and that is where several girls engage in oral sex with the same boy. They put on different shades of lipstick, with the result being a rainbow on the little boy.

DR. LISA MASTERSON (COHOST): Risky behavior.

DR. JIM SEARS (COHOST): And then . . . then the guys, apparently, they . . . they compare to see how many different colors they can have, and—

KAISER: I mean, there's definitely a competition in how many girls you can get, how many different colors you can get.[29]

In most segments devoted to sex bracelets or rainbow parties, the hosts had the final word, and they tended to use it to reaffirm the reality of the risks. Thus, after discussions of sex bracelets, *The Today Show*'s Matt Lauer said, "Just another reason [my daughter is] staying home until she is 23," while *Good Morning America*'s Diane Sawyer concluded by urging parents, "[You] might want to have a talk with your kids."[30]

Closer to Home: Local Coverage

The national coverage of the rainbow-party and sex-bracelet stories did not go unnoticed by local TV stations. In many cases, high-profile national media coverage was followed by local stations covering the same topic. For example, after the *NBC Nightly News* covered the controversy surrounding sexually explicit books for teens, including the novel *Rainbow Party*, at least ten other local stations covered the story in the days that followed.

In total, we found approximately 60 references to sex bracelets and rainbow parties on local U.S. television news programs. These stations were spread all over the country from big-city markets, such as San Diego, Las Vegas, Chicago, Dallas, and New York, to smaller cities, such as Little Rock, Buffalo, Cedar Rapids, Norfolk, and West Palm Beach. Not only do these stations have a combined audience of millions of viewers, but their broadcasts may add further credibility to a story because it is introduced by well-known local media anchors, often alongside other content pertinent to the hometown audience.

Viewers also may have been persuaded of the veracity of these stories by how the message was delivered. Just as national news programs gave sensationalistic teasers to introduce stories on sex bracelets and rainbow parties, local news did the same—with a twist. That is, they embedded stories on sex bracelets and rainbow parties with news accounts of local happenings and other important news stories that had actually been documented, thereby making it more difficult for the viewer to sort fact from legend. Thus, a 2005 report from Huntsville, Alabama, begins,

> Parents, listen up: what your child wears to school could be sending the wrong message. Coming up next at five, we'll tell you more about the so-called sex bracelets—and what they mean. Stay with us. I'm Jerry Hayes with a look at local news. . . . Does your child wear this kind of bracelet? Some say it's more than a trend. The color could be sending the wrong message to their peers. And a local soldier returns home from war to find his business in shambles. We'll have more on these stories coming up tonight on News Channel 19 at five and six.[31]

Similarly, on a New York–area station, a news segment begins by reporting a wildfire in California, covers health news, including information on a scientific research study, and then covers rainbow parties: "Parents, beware: your child may be invited to a rainbow party. How this raunchy social gathering could lead to a social disease."[32] Thus, viewers are seamlessly led from footage of a serious problem in California to a story about scientific research to a report that treats a contemporary legend as fact, without skipping a beat.

TV Shows Get In on the Act

As sex bracelets and rainbow parties became hot topics in the press, the stories started showing up in plot lines of fictional TV shows. We found nine different dramatic programs that covered sex bracelets or rainbow parties between November 2003 and March 2011. What is interesting about these fictional accounts is how closely they mirrored the treatment of these topics in nonfiction TV genres. For example, many news stories issued a "parental alert" claiming that parents were unaware or even "clueless" of the secret behavior of their teenage son or daughter. Similarly, in the first coverage of sex bracelets on a fictional TV series (in November 2003—just months after the story began attracting attention in other media), the plot of an episode of the ABC sitcom *George Lopez* featured Angie, a mother who stumbles on her daughter, Carmen, talking to a friend about sex bracelets. Angie failed to overhear the bracelets' secret meanings and upon seeing the bracelets says to Carmen, "Cute bracelet. You know, a blue one would make a great gift for the flower girl." Carmen replies, "Do not—do that!" Later, Angie likes the bracelets so much she gets some herself and wears them to the grocery store. When she gets home, she takes the scissors to the bracelets and tells her husband what happened while wearing them:

> I had an interesting trip to the grocery store. . . . When the teenage boy bagging my groceries noticed my bracelets, I took it as a compliment. When he helped me to the car, I thought it was really sweet. When he put his hand on my butt and told me he'd never done purple with an older chick, I hit him. When he stopped crying, and we found his retainer, he told me that each of those colors stands for something different you'll do with a boy.

This incident prompts the parents to panic over why their daughter is wearing the bracelets. Carmen reassures them that she wasn't doing what the bracelets mean but wears them because "people think it's cool": "A week ago, hardly anyone at school talked to me. Now everyone likes me."[33]

A year later, in November 2004, on the Showtime drama-comedy *Huff*, the title character and his wife find out that their 14-year-old son has attended—and participated in—a rainbow party. Once again the parents are in the dark and comically stumble on what their son, Bird, is up to. The confrontation begins when Beth, Bird's mother, finds lipstick smeared in his jockey shorts. When both parents confront their son, he confesses that he went to a rainbow party the previous night. The mother does not know what a rainbow party is and mistakenly assumes her son is coming out as gay.

> BETH: A rainbow party? Wow. Bird, I am so glad that you feel safe enough
>   to tell us about this. [*Huff looks puzzled.*] And we'll talk about it, and
>   we'll just keep . . . talking, you know, about it, and I'm sure there's
>   a lot that your father and I need to learn. Honey, we could join
>   PFLAG. . . .
> BIRD: What is PFLAG?
> BETH: Parents for Lesbians and Gays. It's a support group for parents
>   whose children are gay.
> BIRD: What? What are you talking about? I'm not gay.
> BETH: Oh! Uh, but isn't . . . the rainbow a symbol for the gay community?
> BIRD: It's a rainbow *party*. It's a—it's where girls wear lipstick and give guys
>   blow jobs. That's it . . . a blow-job party.
> BETH: A blow-job *party*? There are parties . . . for . . . blow jobs?
> BIRD: Yeah.
> BETH: And . . . and they are called rainbow parties.
> BIRD: Right. They . . . call them that because the guys bring in lipstick and
>   the girls put it on and then give them blow jobs, and the guy with the
>   most colors at the end of the night wins.[34]

Another theme found in the news coverage of sex bracelets was detailing which sex acts the different colors represented. In the television news accounts it was common for journalists or hosts to act shocked by the color codes or to claim that the meanings of one or more of the colors were so deviant that they could not be revealed. This was depicted in some fictional television episodes as well. In a 2005 episode of the popular NBC drama *Law and Order: Special Victims Unit*—known for having story lines that are "ripped from the headlines"—the police investigate the murder of a 15-year-old girl. The officers interview the principal at the school the deceased teen attended:

> PRINCIPAL: The only time I ever had to call [the deceased] in [my office] was over the sex bracelets, and I'm sure that was just peer pressure.
>
> MALE POLICE OFFICER: Sex bracelets?
>
> PRINCIPAL: Different colored bracelets the girls wear, signaling which sex acts they're willing to perform. Uh, yellow's hugging, purple's kissing, red is for a lap dance, blue is for oral sex, and . . . don't make me say what black is for.[35]

Similarly, in a 2005 episode of F/X's drama *Nip/Tuck*, the main characters, who are plastic surgeons, go to a party at a fraternity house and stumble on a sex-bracelet party, which is an unfamiliar concept to them. One of the doctors asks a fraternity brother what the bracelets are for. The fraternity brother replies, "Ahh, it's a bracelet party. They're color coded. See, every girl wears whichever color they're looking for tonight—like blue means they like head, double blue means they like 69, pink means they're into girls too—sort of streamlines the whole process." The doctor responds by asking if there is a bracelet for girls who like guys twice their age. The fraternity brother answers, "Green—means they like money!"[36]

Another theme from the television news coverage of sex bracelets and rainbow parties that several fictional shows picked up on was that kids today engage in sex—or think about sex—too casually. In the same episode of *Huff* mentioned earlier, Beth tells her husband, "[Our son is] getting blow jobs in the same nonchalant way that you and I used to go to the movies."[37] Similarly, a couple of episodes depict adults being shocked that contemporary teens do not think of oral sex as "sex." For example, in an October 2004 episode of the CBS drama *Judging Amy*, the title character is presiding over a sexual-assault case. The episode examines a case of unwanted oral sex in which the defendant (Brent) allegedly demanded that the plaintiff (Caroline) perform oral sex on him. The defendant claims he did so because the girl in question was wearing a blue jelly bracelet, which supposedly signified willingness to engage in oral sex. While on the stand, the defendant has the following exchange with the judge:

BRENT: [People] go to the party to hook up, do what every girl's up for. Most of them don't even want real sex.

JUDGE: Real sex?

BRENT: They just want to fool around, you know?

JUDGE: No, I'm pretty sure I don't know. What does fooling around mean to you?

BRENT: Kissing . . . to . . . to everything but. . . . When the guys saw Caroline's blue bracelet, they started to say stuff.

JUDGE: Her blue bracelet?

BRENT: Yeah, the girls wear these, uh—I don't know what you call them —jelly bracelets? They come in different colors, so you know what they're into. And blue means they do oral sex.

JUDGE: Girls color code themselves?

BRENT: Orange is just kissing, black means they go all the way, and . . . and clear's wild card. . . . I never saw a clear.[38]

Some news coverage of sex bracelets and rainbow parties focused particularly on the behavior of girls today compared to girls from previous generations. In news accounts, this concern takes the form of debates over what has caused this supposed change in behavior. In fictional accounts, the concern is dramatized by portraying girls behaving in a sexually aggressive manner. In the *Nip/Tuck* episode mentioned earlier, a college girl approaches one of the older plastic surgeons at the fraternity party. The doctor asks her what her braided bracelet means. She replies, "That means for the right guy, I do anything."[39]

A 2010 episode of *The Hard Times of RJ Berger*, which aired on MTV, picked up on this theme of female promiscuity in a scene in which characters discuss whether even girls who claim to be "pure" really are. The sequence begins with the title character and his friend Miles sitting together on the school bus. RJ, who is a virgin, wants to have sex with a new girl in school, but he's learned she wears a purity ring. The episode comically examines whether purity is all it is cracked up to be.

MILES: You ever heard of a rainbow party?

RJ: No.

MILES: Well, the purity kids invented them. They're also called everything-but parties, because it's everything but sex—you know, like butt sex, like *butt* with two *t*'s—

RJ: I get it.

MILES: See, that's how they stay technically pure, by saving the baby hole for the Lord.

RJ: So what goes down at these parties?

MILES: Girls, RJ, girls do. Apparently there's a punch bowl filled with lipsticks, all the colors of the rainbow. The goal is for each girl to leave a color on as many guys as possible. When they're done, each girl's left her mark, and by keeping the front door nailed shut, they've done it all with God's approval.[40]

Many television dramas try to stay current and relevant to their audience by reflecting what is happening in real life. Given that sex bracelets and rainbow parties were the subject of much media coverage, it is not surprising that they began showing up in the plots of fictional programs. However, like TV's nonfiction genres, these dramas treated these stories as factual, forms of sexual play that are commonly known among today's kids yet below the radar of adults. These story lines seem to underscore the notion that the teens' sexual behavior is more outrageous than ever before. The possibility that these tales were best viewed as contemporary legends, that they ought to be treated with a degree of skepticism, was never raised.

Becoming Cultural Touchstones

Television news coverage exposed millions of people to stories about sex bracelets and rainbow parties. Since various forms of media borrow stories from one another, television coverage played an integral part in spreading these stories; as of late 2012, sex bracelets continued to receive media attention in countries all over the world, including England, Ireland, Australia, and Brazil. It is not surprising that television comedies and dramas borrowed from current topics in the news and thereby added to the exposure that sex bracelets and rainbow parties received.

In the wake of all this media attention, these stories began to be referenced on television without any further explanation. Sex bracelets and rainbow parties had become cultural touchstones. In other words, it was apparently assumed that these stories had become common knowledge or that at least many people would get the reference. For example, on a 2010 episode of CNN's *Joy Behar Show*, the host interviewed comedienne Kathy Griffin about her plan to broadcast her annual gynecological exam.

> BEHAR: You know, I can't understand [women's reluctance to get pap smears], because in my day a lot of the girls were virgins, believe it or not. But the younger girls, these girls are sleeping around like crazy now; this is no big deal, believe me. . . .
>
> GRIFFIN: Yes, this is nothing compared to a rainbow party.
>
> BEHAR: Exactly.[41]

Note how both women understand the reference. Similarly, on a 2012 episode of NBC's *The Today Show*, cohosts Kathie Lee Gifford and Hoda Kotb showed a clip from the movie *American Reunion*, in which rainbow parties are referenced. In the clip, one male character says, "Okay, is it just me or do girls today seem a bit sluttier?" The other male character replies, "Oh, definitely. Teen sex, rainbow parties, sexting nude photos—saw it all on Kathie Lee and Hoda." Following the clip, Gifford responded by saying, "Well, we are here to inform the public, so . . ."[42]

Likewise, producers of television dramas have apparently come to believe that merely showing sex bracelets or tubes of lipstick near a teen party is sufficient to make their point. In a 2010 episode of CBS's hit show *The Good Wife*, a young girl, who is interested in the teenage son of the title character and her politician husband, is wearing a wrist full of jelly bracelets. The bracelets are not explained; instead, the young girl says. "Hey, I like politicians' kids. What can I say?" As the camera focuses on her bracelet-filled wrist, she continues, "I need one more to complete my political education."[43]

But the clearest use of these stories as cultural touchstones—and the clearest example of skepticism regarding these tales on TV—comes from a 2010 *Saturday Night Live* skit featuring a news anchor introducing a story about "another terrifying teenage trend," followed by a trench-coated reporter describing *trampolining*: "A teen boy sits on the roof of a one-story house receiving oral sex from a girl jumping up and down on a large backyard trampoline. Sources say if a girl trampolines ten boys, she receives a bracelet—and that's what Silly Bandz are." The skit went on to show a teenager calmly dismissing the reporter's questions about trampolining ("I've never done this. . . . I don't think that's even physically possible"), while her mother is overcome by hysterical fear.[44] The skit managed to combine the oral sex of rainbow parties with the bracelet-as-coupon theme of sex bracelets and to illustrate how television uncritically promotes concern and the public gets caught up in fear. Satire, then, permitted a critical reflection of television's coverage of these stories that was otherwise absent when TV addressed claims about sex bracelets and rainbow parties.

While this chapter examines television's role in spreading the contemporary legends about sex bracelets and rainbow parties, these are only two among many claims about teen sex that have received a great deal of media attention in recent years. For example, in 2008, *Time* magazine ran a piece about a high school in Massachusetts where there had been an increase in student pregnancies and quoted the school principal, who claimed that the girls had made a pact to get pregnant together. Following this story, there was an onslaught of media coverage citing the so-called pregnancy pact as another piece of evidence that teens were out of control. This story made headlines in the U.S. as well as in Australia, Canada, England, Ireland, and Scotland. Later, some reports cast doubt on whether there ever was such a pact (apparently, the principal who claimed there was a pact could not remember where he heard that information, and nobody else could confirm his version of the story). Yet news coverage persisted, and in 2010, a made-for-television movie, *The Pregnancy Pact*, was released on the Lifetime cable channel, which claimed it was "inspired by a true story."[45]

For the pregnancy-pact story, like reports of sex bracelets and rainbow parties, the pattern is clear. The media picks up a salacious story: sexual topics tend to be newsworthy; in particular, stories about kids and sex are especially newsworthy because they can be approached from various angles—vulnerable kids in danger of victimization and needing protection, licentious kids, especially girls, gone wild and needing to be brought under control, middle-class kids acting out as much as kids from the "wrong side of the tracks," and so on. While print media sometimes offer nuanced treatments that allow critics and skeptics to be heard, television's attention tends to be more fleeting and less subtle. When TV did cover rainbow parties or sex bracelets, it rarely lasted more than a few minutes—a short segment in a longer program. Presumably, this reflected the limited material TV had to work with: there was no footage of sexual play, no detailed testimony from kids who acknowledged participating in these activities, no experts who had studied the subjects. Instead, TV coverage came down to repeating the legends. There is not much difference between Oprah hosting a writer who said that she talked to girls who said they'd heard about rainbow parties and conversations in which people relay what they've heard from someone who knows someone who knows a person who had sex after breaking a bracelet. But television's larger audiences mean that these stories spread further, until they become familiar cultural touch-stones, just one of those things everybody knows about kids today. As a result, not only do the legends become commonly believed, but the "teens gone wild" image becomes ingrained. This, in turn, affects how we think about the overall image of today's young people.

4

Online Conversations about Kids and Sex

You will never find the elusive girls that do this kind of thing
outside the imaginations of teen boys.
—Morrison's Lament, post on NFBSK, 2004

Clearly television and other media love stories about kids running wild.
Recall Oprah's guest warning that rainbow parties were "pervasive" or
the headline in the UK's *Sun* about the "Bracelet Which Means Your
Child Is Having SEX."[1] In terms of their potential to command an audience's attention, these were effective news stories: they were disturbing,
shocking, memorable. This coverage inspired considerable online commentary among members of the larger public. However, whereas most
television reports uncritically supported claims about rainbow parties
and sex bracelets, the people who responded to these stories online
expressed a wider range of views.

As we have noted, folklorists envision legends as being transmitted
by word of mouth, through face-to-face performances, in which someone tells a tale to one or more listeners. But our data derive from online
posts; most of these comments were not examples of someone repeating
a legend so much as reactions to the stories.[2] Some of these comments
were posted as blogs or website pages, so they are the work of people
who may have a more-than-passing presence on the web, but the vast
majority were amateur comments, posted by individuals in response to

something they read on the web, such as a news report, a query, or a comment in a discussion thread. The format for these discussions was fundamentally interactive, with people exchanging views and often disagreeing with one another. Unlike the face-to-face, teller-dominated performances in which folklorists envision most legends being told, these online conversations involved more people actively engaged in the discussions and more open disagreement and debate. These comments can be viewed as reflecting the range of sentiments found among the general public.

Online comments pose problems for analysts. Social scientists who use interviews, observation, and other methods of collecting data must always be aware that their research subjects may lie, distort, exaggerate, or dissemble. However, it can be particularly difficult to know how online comments should be interpreted. It is impossible to know for certain whether posted comments are sincere, that is, whether an individual is telling the truth or at least believes a comment to be true, whether a particular comment is intended to be taken literally or is a bit of intentional exaggeration or sarcasm, or even whether the individual making the comment is the sort of person he or she purports to be or is misrepresenting such basic facts as his or her age or gender.

However, this chapter is not trying to determine the truth of various online comments about rainbow parties and sex bracelets so much as it seeks to understand the different sorts of claims that people made in discussing these topics. At bottom, these online conversations can be viewed as debates over whether sex play prompted by rainbow parties or sex bracelets posed a social problem. Some people accepted the truth of these stories, while others doubted the tales, and both believers and skeptics tried to make the case for their views. This chapter seeks to describe this debate, to examine the sorts of evidence and reasoning ordinary individuals use when trying to make sense of contemporary legends. We summarize online discussions; overall, these involved hundreds of different people making hundreds of comments, on dozens of online forums that seemed to attract different sorts of

participants, including sites for youths, political and religious conservatives, parents, readers of particular newspapers, skeptics, and so on. All
manner of topics were raised in these discussions, but many comments
debated whether rainbow parties and sex bracelets were important
social phenomena.

In order to bring some order to this confusion, we begin with some
broad generalizations about two basic stances individuals adopted:
belief versus skepticism. In general, *believers* accepted the truth of these
reports; that is, they believed that some young people were participating
in rainbow parties or that they were using sex bracelets as sexual props.
Believers understood these practices to be new, troubling developments
that endangered both the kids involved and the larger society's future.

In contrast, *skeptics* did not consider the reports convincing; they
were the ones who tended to dismiss these stories as urban legends, by
which they meant that these were "just" stories, that there was no—or
at least very little—truth to them, so that people did not need to worry
about rainbow parties or sex bracelets.

In other words, much of the online debate about rainbow parties and
sex bracelets focused on whether the reports of these phenomena were
true or whether they were urban legends (and therefore false). Note
that framing the distinction this way ignores folklorists' understanding of legends as stories that spread informally; folklorists view a story's
truth as irrelevant to whether it should be classified as a legend. But the
popular understanding of legend (discussed in chapter 2) assumes that
a legend is false. Taken to its logical extreme, this stance poses problems. Once we assume that a legend is completely false, a claim that
a story is a legend can be understood to mean that the story must be
absolutely untrue, so that even one bit of evidence that there is truth
to the story would disqualify the tale from being classified as a legend.
In this view, a single case of a rainbow party having occurred—or of a
sex bracelet leading to serious sexual activity—might be understood as
proof that the story was no mere legend. Moreover, because one cannot
prove a negative—that is, it is impossible to demonstrate that there has

never been a rainbow party or a single instance of a broken sex brace-let leading to serious sexual behavior—it is theoretically impossible to demonstrate that something is an urban legend (if we take that to mean a completely false story).

In practice, the standards people used when debating these stories online were somewhat more flexible. The believers who warned about rainbow parties and sex bracelets argued that these were relatively common practices (recall that Oprah's guest claimed that rainbow parties were "pervasive"). But just what this might mean in practice was unclear. Did pervasive mean that 1 in 100 teens had participated in rainbow par-ties? One in 1,000? In 10,000? In 100,000? Similarly, while skeptics could not prove that these things had never happened, they did argue that they were uncommon. That is, in calling these tales urban legends, they meant that the stories greatly exaggerated any threats posed by rainbow parties and sex bracelets. Yet, again, there was no clear stan-dard for how rare something needed to be to be considered uncommon.

Classifying Online Comments

The online debate about these sexual practices generally involved be-lievers arguing that they were disturbingly common among kids, while skeptics countered that they were relatively rare. Within this general framework, individuals contributed various sorts of evidence or rea-soned arguments to support their views. The remainder of this chapter explores the sorts of things they had to say. It is organized around differ-ent types of arguments and evidence that people invoked to make their cases—first-person testimony, secondhand accounts, and so on. As the chapter proceeds, it will become clear that most types of arguments mirrored parallel, opposing claims, so that both believers and skeptics presented first-person accounts and so on. In order to give the flavor of these discussions, we will quote many examples of these claims. Again, we emphasize that these are verbatim quotations; in order to convey a sense of the nature of online conversations, we have not corrected errors in spelling, grammar, and so on.[3] Although our sample contained about five times more comments about sex bracelets than about rainbow parties, we have made an effort to use illustrations from both debates, in order to demonstrate that similar sorts of reasoning shaped both discussions. And because it isn't always clear whether a particular excerpt refers to rainbow parties or sex bracelets, each quotation will be preceded by an identifying code. Thus, "[RP1]" identifies the first quote about rainbow parties, while "[SB10]" stands for the tenth quote about sex bracelets.

Firsthand Reports

As we saw in chapter 3, television coverage tended to involve adults relaying claims about rainbow parties and sex bracelets. But many of the people who participated in online discussions presented themselves as youths who claimed to have a better sense of the truth about rainbow parties or sex bracelets than could be had by the adults reporting for the media. Some of these individuals offered firsthand accounts; that is, they described personal experiences that spoke to the truth or falsity of the stories.

Believers. Some comments offered firsthand observations that seemed to affirm the stories' truth, although without the person making the comment claiming direct involvement in sexual activities:

[RP1] When I was a junior in high school I was in with the in group and we had these parties once or twice a month.[4]

[SB1] im in 8th grade. . . . i have an arm full of them but i dont let people snap them but my friends do and lets just say im the only virgin in my group i wont let any one even nea my arms but its fun to have guys try to get to them i have let a guy snap a yellow one which means a hug and thats it but sex braacelets are no myth i promise.[5]

[SB2] im only 12 and i have lots of sex bracelets and yes i consider them SEX bracelets and alot of parents should be scared.[6]

Other firsthand comments offered more detail, although these often depicted practices that were less extreme or less shocking than the versions conveyed by the media:

[RP2] I actully went to one last weekend. But many teens change it to any exposed skin, not guys dicks. Also, its usually a person kissing the person they like, or are intressed in.[7]

[RP3] When I was 17 I participated in a few (well 2 to be exact) And it doesn't happen the way they are saying it does. It's more disclosed than that. None of us got BJ's in front of everyone it was always in a bathroom, closet or other non-public place. The first party I went to, I only got one shade, but the second one, I got 3 colors.[8]

[SB3] im 13 and trust me these jelly bracelets do have meanings i know this cause some boy broke my glittery clear one and he grabed my ass.[9]

A few firsthand claims were indeed dramatic but sometimes smacked of braggadocio:

[SB4] the sexist girl in my year snapped my black 1 lets just say we needed rubbers by the way im in 1st year.[10]

[SB5] i accidentally broke a black one and it was really fun!!!!!! if you know what i mean!!!![11]

Such claims of firsthand experience were themselves greeted with skepticism by other commentators (e.g., [RP4] "Ah, here come the netsibishionists . . .").[12] In any case, first-person accounts confirming the basic truth of stories about rainbow parties and sex bracelets were not common; only about 15—less than 1%—of the comments in our sample offered this sort of testimony.

Skeptics. In contrast, there were far more—well over 100—comments from individuals who invoked their firsthand experiences with sex bracelets to cast doubt on the stories. Most of these were posted by youths. Some said that they did not attribute any sexual meanings to the bracelets, that they simply wore them for fashion. Others acknowledged that the bracelets were widely understood to have sexual meanings yet denied that they in fact led to much sexual behavior:

[SB6] I have had one snapped yes and all I did was laugh and the guy didn't bother me about it he was just like haha I broke it what does that one mean . . . I told him and he laughed then walked away . . . he thought nothing of it . . .[13]

[SB7] Hey, I'm 13 And Yeah We Wear Those Bracelets And Everyone Knows The Sexual Meanings. We Sort Of Take It Seriously, But Not Completly. Like If Someone Snaps it, We All Just snicker and Go Eww you have to have sex with so and so Sure It's A Little Juvinille but it's kind of fun as a joke. the fartest we go is kissing.[14]

[SB8] These bands are meaningless. I know people from 12 to 17 who wear them, so I've seen a fair few snapped off of the girls wrists. Not a single sexual act was performed because of it. The guys, well everytime they lost one they'd say something had happened, but I wonder how may guys simple broke their own at home and made a story . . .[15]

There were fewer comments about rainbow parties, but there were first-person accounts that were skeptical:

[RP5] I judge false. I am a freshman and yes I agree, kids are having sex, reciving and giving oral, sence the earlyest that i remember, 7th grade.

But these are only select individuals. I am considered a fairly atractive guy in my school, and I can say truthfuly the furthest I've gotten with any girl was some finger play, and that was on only one occasion and was just a little playing around.[16]

[RP6] Speaking as someone who went to high school in Colorado as late as 9 years ago, I can assure you that I saw NOTHING of this sort. The Colorado high school parties I went to were the run-of-the mill, 20 guys trying desperately to get laid, and 5 or 6 girls having none of it.[17]

The great majority of first-person accounts were skeptical. But of course someone denying having participated in sexual activities related to rainbow parties or sex bracelets cannot be taken as proof that no other person has had such experiences.

Secondhand Reports

Probably the most common way for someone telling a contemporary legend to make the story seem credible is to identify the person to whom the events happened: "This didn't happen to me, but it happened to my brother's barber." Folklorists use the term *FOAF* (a friend of a friend) for such attributions.[18] Not surprisingly, our sample contains numerous comments written by people providing secondhand information.

Believers. Some comments posted by young people invoke a friend's claims of having had sexual experiences with rainbow parties or sex bracelets:

[SB9] one of my friends has every color and almost all of them are broken now!! she has done all of the request! . . . Im 11 and in 6th grade!!! trust me i know!!!!!!!![19]

[RP7] I know rainbow parties exist for a fact. Though I realy haven't been to one, I know my best friend has, and she isn't lying. She showed me all her lipsticks too.[20]

[RP8] I am a sexual health counselor and I have heard specific incidents from my clients who have participated in these parties.[21]

Other comments offered fewer specifics but involved claims of knowing youths who were in the know and therefore, in all probability, were involved:

[RP9] I have heard of this several months ago from a group of kids talking about what they heard at school about one. Kids are ruthless these days. Not a doubt in my mind that they exist.[22]

Some comments argued that while knowing people who knew of the story was evidence that it was probably true, secondhand denials of involvement could not be trusted:

[SB10] Even if they do consider them sex bracelets . . . it's highly unlikely they would admit it to you anyways so you can't really say that for sure.[23]

[RP10] I have tried speaking to a few youngsters and surprisingly, almost half of them have heard of it. But none told me that they had indulged in it . . . Yeah, right![24]

In other words, while some believers invoked secondhand reports as evidence of the stories' truth, others drew the same conclusions from secondhand denials.

Skeptics. Skeptics argued that there was little firsthand evidence of these sexual practices. Alex commented on the Museum of Hoaxes website,

"[RP11] Tales about rainbow parties always seem to be third-hand: coming from adults who are trying to raise alarms about teenage sexuality."[25] Just as there were lots of first-person denials, there were second-hand claims that the person making the comment knew people who weren't involved:

> [SB11] my friend wears tons of em and she aint neverr donee any dat crap . . .[26]

> [SB12] two of my best mates wear shag bands and even if they do get snapped, they don't do the shit u guys are on about. They know full well what each band means but they just wear them as a fashion icon.[27]

Sex bracelets in particular seemed to offer the basis for new second-hand tales that hinted at the amusing possibilities inherent in the bracelets' ambiguous meanings:

> [SB13] Everyone is wearing' them at school + i'm only 13. One teacher told this boy to take them off but he sorta couldn't he was trying to take 'em off without breaking 'em + he goes "don't snap them miss."[28]

> [SB14] Everyone is wearing them at my school and one of my mates asked a teacher to snap a black one = sex lol and he did lol.[29]

These stories about teachers—like many of the first- and secondhand skeptical accounts that described kids teasing one another about sex bracelets—traded on playful ambiguity: What if one person understands what a bracelet means and another does not? What if they both are in the know, and a bracelet gets broken? These skeptical comments portrayed sex bracelets as exciting because they straddled the boundary between childlike innocence and sexual knowledge, and they provided opportunities for kids to play at transgression and to display poise.

The Relevance of Media Coverage

Chapter 2 demonstrated that the media played an important role in drawing broad attention to both stories. Both believers and skeptics acknowledged the importance of media coverage, although they interpreted its significance in very different ways.

Believers. Believers pointed to media coverage as evidence that rainbow parties and sex bracelets led to real, dangerous sexual practices. One of the earliest web-based comments, a November 2003 piece in the *Education Coffeehouse Newsletter*, dismissed claims by some parents and students that sex bracelets weren't a big deal by noting that the story had been "[SB15] revealed by one of the most trustworthy sources in journalism—Time Magazine."[30] Other believers' comments made parallel claims citing different pieces of media coverage:

> [RP11] I just graduated High School two years ago and I know for a fact these things are real!!! I never did them. . . . But there were girls who did. . . . Read Jodi Picoult's book The Tenth Circle.[31]

> [SB16] Judging Amy did have an episode about this issue, and the court cases in that series were all based on real cases. How serious it was in real life, is a guess.[32]

> [SB17] Oprah covered this with girls who were "into it." They were positively glowing about all the action.[33]

For believers, coverage in a range of media, from journalism (newspapers and newsmagazines), infotainment (talk shows), and even outright entertainment (novels and TV dramas) affirmed the reality of the rainbow-party and sex-bracelet stories.

Skeptics. Skeptics dismissed the same media sources that believers treated as authoritative as unreliable. Thus, a comment that referenced

Oprah's coverage as evidence of the reality of rainbow parties received the sarcastic response, "[RP12] Yes, because shows like this are perfect ways to determine what is *really* going on in the world."[34] Other skeptics suggested that media coverage had disseminated knowledge of the stories and could be blamed both for exaggerated public concern and for much of whatever sexual activity might have occurred:

> [SB18] The thing is, before the news story about this "trend" broke, there was no trend.[35]

> [SB19] We never even heard of sex braceltes here until doctor phil had it on his show.[36]

> [RP13] Contrary to popular belief, this was not a term made up by Oprah, it was brought about in a juvenille fiction book called "Rainbow Party."[37]

For some skeptics, these stories reflected poor journalistic practices. They characterized coverage as "[SB20] media hype"[38] or "[SB21] Rubbish Journalism at its finest!"[39] In this view, media coverage of rainbow parties and shag bands resembled other coverage that blew topics out of proportion: "[SB22] This sounds like exactly the sort of bogus non-story that the media would jump all over and try to exaggerate to absurd proportions."[40]

The Believers' Rejoinders. Some believers dismissed skeptics' claims that the stories were simply scares promoted by the media:

> [RP11] I have no problem believing that they are true, and I'm only in my early 20's. The young kids that think that Oprah made this up to trick parents is nonsense. Kids are getting sexually active younger and younger doing things like blowing an entire JV football team.[41]

> [RP12] I had a good amount of girls in my class, year 2000, come up to ask if I wanted to join. . . . Never even heard of Oprah talking about

it, and neither had any of these girls. I assure you, Oprah did not make it up![42]

Although believers and skeptics interpreted the media's influence in different ways, their comments reveal the media's centrality to the spread of these legends. Many comments reveal awareness of what the media say, and this knowledge could be used either to affirm a story or to call it into question.

Marketing Sex Bracelets

Believers and skeptics, then, argued about the media's role in drawing attention to both rainbow parties and sex bracelets. In the case of sex bracelets, online comments also debated the impact of another institution: business. Although performing both rainbow parties and sex bracelets required some special equipment, the colored lipsticks implicated in rainbow parties were considered common, everyday cosmetics; possessing or applying lipstick was not considered telling. Sex bracelets were another matter. Discussions of shag bands often began by explaining what constituted a sex bracelet and distinguishing them from other rubbery bracelets, like the colored wristbands used to raise funds for or convey concern about cancer awareness and other causes or the Silly Bandz that assumed various shapes when removed from the wearer's wrist. The confusion was enhanced by some people using the term *sex bracelets* as a generic term for gel bracelets. Thus, a site for one bracelet vendor featured a page headed "Sex Bracelets and Their Meaning," illustrated with a photo of four colored wristbands bearing the slogan "I AM THE RESURRECTION," that offered this recommendation: "[SB23] So for your next family gathering, office party, personal or surprise gift or choice of promotional products with distinction, choose sex bracelets and their meaning to be unique, stand out and still be trendy!!"[43]

But even when believers defined sex bracelets narrowly, they worried about the motives of the businesses that sold these products, in some cases offering embellished accounts that demonstrated business's culpability:

> [SB24] This is probably some right wing lard arses idea to make money.[44]

> [SB25] some come with printouts about which is which.[45]

> [SB26] It is horrid and companies that make profit off exploiting the children in such ways should definitely be forced to pay penalties, though I can see some high priced lawyer saying "They are marketed to adults, if children got a hold of them the parents should be held accountable."[46]

Skeptics countered that the bracelets had been around for years and that kids had only recently invested them with sexual meanings:

> [SB27] How the heck can you prove that the other companies made it for sexual acts? I am not saying that businesses are not capable of sick things as such but let's not forget once again that the kids started this. Should we just start outlawing everything kids turn into a sexual game?[47]

Of course, debates over social issues often revolve around the role of business—just as they often address the role of media. It is not uncommon for some people to argue that media and business cause or at least exacerbate social problems and for others to defend those institutions. In online comments, people borrowed these familiar lines of reasoning and applied them to rainbow parties and sex bracelets.

Social Change

Another familiar theme in debates about social issues is ongoing social change. That is, people interpret topics such as rainbow parties and sex bracelets in relation to how they understand society to be changing.

Believers. Many believers insisted that today's young people are far more sexually knowledgeable and experienced than were previous generations. They contrasted the relative innocence of the past with the more explicit sexuality represented by rainbow parties and sex bracelets:

[SB28] So scarey—the worst we had at primary school was kiss, cuddle or torture and we thought that was risque back then.[48]

[RP13] I just can't understand how much things have changed since I was a kid. . . . The most we ever did was make out in a dark closet. Now look what kids are doing. It' absolutely mind blowing.[49]

[SB29] This is a natural extension of the sexual revolution. It was only a matter of time before it filtered down to 11 year old girls.[50]

[SB30] Its crazy this stuff was happening at my middle school in NC. . . . Can you beleive that kids were having *sex* in the school auditorium.[51]

What accounted for these developments? A number of comments referenced Bill Clinton, presumably because the Lewinsky scandal had led to public discussions about oral sex.[52] Others identified a range of developments—often linked to other social problems—as contributing to kids' sexual activities:

[SB31] All the hormones in the food is making kids become adults faster . . . I blame the meat and the dairy industry.[53]

[SB32] Kids know about sex at a younger age simply because everywhere they turn it's right in front of them. It's not a kids fault that we use sex to sell things, it's our fault.[54]

[SB33] There is an epidemic of gonorrhea and STD's of the throat in many inner cities, seems the girls who are inducted into gangs must be initiated and perform.[55]

[RP14] I have to point out that this type of thing is probably more likely to happen than you would believe. While I'm not really sure if these are really organized lipstick gatherings, you must keep in mind that there are ALOT of young girls out there with low self esteem, weight problems, and certain family issues who have no problems at all with group sex.[56]

Believers, then, linked all sorts of social changes to these stories; in their view, these developments offered a context that made tales of rainbow parties and sex bracelets seem plausible.

Skeptics. Skeptics, in contrast, viewed claims that rainbow parties and sex bracelets represented dramatic social changes as exaggerated. They argued that while it was possible, perhaps even probable, that there had been some instances of sexual activity, even if there was a bit of truth to the stories, this did not necessarily constitute a serious social problem:

[RP14] Totally a myth. That's not to say that something like it hasn't happened at some point, somewhere. But to say it's a trend, or that it's happening all the time, is completely false in my opinion.[57]

[RP15] I'm not saying that these "rainbow parties" are some sort of rampant epidemic. The vast majority of kids certainly aren't involved in this type of thing. However, I have no doubt that where there is smoke there is at least some fire.[58]

[SB34] It's all part of the "well, this generation is going to hell" ranting that has been going on since Ancient Greek times.[59]

Other skeptics conceded that today's youth might participate in rainbow parties or sex bracelets, but they suggested that this might be a good thing. Several made jokes contrasting the constraints on their own youthful sexuality with the alleged freedom of today's kids:

[SB35] I wish it were that easy when I was in high school—back then we had to find the easy girls the hard way.[60]

A slightly different claim was that sexual play might be good for teens:

[SB36] Let the kids play, I say. Better educated now, than becoming some deprived sex monsters later in life.[61]

However, a far more common skeptical response argued that the change represented by rainbow parties and sex bracelets was illusionary. Dozens of comments pointed to parallels between these stories and tales that were current among earlier cohorts of young people:

[RP16] I remember back when I was in junior high. F**k tabs were the big thing. You'd take the tab off a pop can, and how it broke would determinge what sexual favour you'd get from a girl for it. Of course, the one thing we all knew was that no matter how many tabs you gave a girl, you'd never get anything in return. If something was going to happen, it had nothing to do with the tabs.[62]

[SB37] I had almost forgotten about the pull-tabs: that was popular when I was in junior high and high school, but no one ever had sex or even kissed someone just because they were presented with one—at most it was just a joke between people who were already involved.[63]

These comments reasoned that, if earlier stories about sexual play were false, it was likely there wasn't any more substance to tales of rainbow parties and sex bracelets. Assorted comments recalled school days when sexual meanings were assigned to green M&Ms, beer-bottle labels, earrings, bandanas, shoelaces, particular colors worn on specific days of the week, hair ribbons, whether a watch was worn on the left or right wrist, and so on.

Because the stories about rainbow parties and sex bracelets emerged at roughly the same time, different individuals encountered one story before learning of the other, so that it was possible for a commenter about sex bracelets to remark, "[SB38] all this brouhaha is an awful lot like the 'rainbow party' commotion of a few years ago,"[64] while a discussion thread about rainbow parties included a note that "[RP17] it's just like those 'sex bracelets.' "[65] That is, regardless of which story they heard first, recalling that story and having come to consider that alarm exaggerated, skeptics found it easier to doubt the second tale they heard. All these comments implied that, since earlier, parallel stories about kids' secret sexual customs were exaggerated, it seemed likely that the current stories also lacked substance.

There were also efforts to correct or clarify the history of sex bracelets, as some skeptics argued that this was not a new phenomenon (and hence need not be a cause for alarm). Thus, a 2009 post stated,

[SB39] It is true that Shagbands or Jelly Bracelets used to be an 80's fashion. However, they weren't the original fuck bracelets. Originally fuck bracelets were bracelets with teeny tiny little beads and thin elastic string. The rumours about breaking them and the person has to have sex with you started floating around when I was thirteen. I'm about 17 now.[66]

Still other comments recalled sex bracelets being popular at much earlier times. An Australian discussion thread contained more than a dozen such recollections:

[SB40] This is NOT a new phenomenon—I am 30 years old and these were around when I was a kid.[67]

[SB41] These things were doing the rounds of the high schools in the eighties.[68]

Such comments suggested that, if there was nothing new about sex bracelets, there was no reason to treat the story as alarming news. Skeptics sought to put these concerns in perspective, with reminders ("[SB42] Schools and parents get worked up about fictional horrors all the time")[69] and cautions ("[SB43] Don't get caught up in the moral panic!!!").[70]

Assessing Probabilities

Although believers could point to some evidence to support claims that rainbow parties and sex bracelets were actually leading to sexual activities among young people, skeptics could counter that there wasn't all that much evidence. This led to various attempts to characterize the likelihood that these were serious problems.

Believers. Believers displayed different degrees of confidence in the correctness of their beliefs. At one extreme were those who seemed to insist that these were real phenomena:

> [SB44] If girls wear one of theses bracelets, it means they are willing to perform certain acts. . . . (As a note: This is EXACTLY what the description says. NO girl of any age has EVER worn a jelly bracelet unless she has performed the following. These are the facts, and they cannot be disputed.)[71]

Other believers argued that knowledge of rainbow parties and sex bracelets made sexual activities likely:

> [SB45] Well, give it a couple of weeks. The Genie is out of the bottle.[72]

> [SB46] children follow other children, brought up with wrong morals some children go to far.[73]

Still others insisted that it was at least possible that the stories might be—or might become—true:

[RP18] It may have started out fake, but give it enough time and someone, somewhere, is probably going to be inspired to make it real.[74]

[SB47] The problem is, it temps people into seeing if they will. If they do not, they may be the attack of teasing for being weak.[75]

Perhaps the lowest level of conviction displayed by believers was found in comments that responded to claims that these stories had been debunked on Snopes.com or other urban-legend websites. These comments insisted that it was at least possible that the stories were true:

[SB48] When Snopes calls it "undetermined," I don't dismiss it as an urban legend.[76]

[SB49] Stuff like this isn't proven or debunked. It isn't a single source that can be proven wrong, its a fad that could start today if two kids do it.[77]

Skeptics. Whereas believers argued that the rainbow-party and shag-band stories were plausible, skeptics argued that these tales lacked plausibility. Concerns about rainbow parties led skeptics to note a number of rather practical objections. A journalist argued that "the current oral-sex hysteria . . . presupposes not only that a limitless number of young American girls have taken on the sexual practices of porn queens but also that American boys are capable of having an infinite number of sexual experiences in rapid succession."[78] Online comments raised lots of other issues:

[RP19] If you imagine the motion of proper oral sex, you'll be aware of a lot of "up and down" or "in and out" motion. If one girl with lipstick on is "finished" with a guy, you're not left with a single round circle around the base of the penis, but probably with a "solid colour" penis. And by the time the second girl is done, she probable "washed off" the first girl's mark . . . The "purpose" of the Rainbow Party is supposedly to see which guy gathers the most amount of different colours on his penis . . . I simply cannot imagine a bunch of straight guys whipping out their dicks in front of each other, and examining each other's dicks to look at the different colours . . .[79]

[RP20] How do the girls know what color lipstick to wear? Is there a committee? Do they hand it out at the party? Who buys it? How do they determine the order? Who picks the guy? Can 7 High School girls really agree on anything? Can one High School guy really get 7 girls to blow him? Aren't Teenagers usually pretty jeolous? No, the practicalities of this don't work out. I seriously doubt this is something that happens much. And even when it does, the 7-to-1 female/male ratio seems . . . optimistic.[80]

While comments about rainbow parties invited elaborate speculation about practical arrangements, skeptics' comments about sex bracelets tended to be dismissive:

[SB50] who wears a bracelet after they've had sex? oohhh i just had sex, lemme get out my bracelet color code sheet! please. most people already know when you've had sex, there's no need to parade it around with a bracelet.[81]

[SB51] I have always been skeptical of this story because, suppose a fat smelly loser with thick glasses gets the black bracelet . . . I'm thinking this doesn't work even for the sluttiest girls.[82]

Evidence

In the debate over rainbow parties, skeptics argued that the absence of more evidence was telling. If these parties actually occurred, there should be a better record:

[RP21] If Rainbow Parties were real you could bet your ass that

1. The Porn industry would have cashed in on the idea.

2. Some horny teen dude would post a pick of his rainbow penis to show of his "successful conquest" . . .[83]

[RP22] Several teens have videoed themselves committting acts of vandalsim and other stupidity: By now, if these parties were real, someone would have made a recording of some sort. That would constitute proof.[84]

[SB52] The very fact that everyone actually interviewed about it says they've never heard of it or it's all BS will just be proof that we're all deliberately denying it.[85] [Compare RP10.]

Although there were a few instances of individuals offering first-hand accounts of participating in rainbow parties, these reports also encountered skepticism: "[RP23, in response to RP1] The ones who brag the most get the least. Unless you can provide proof I suggest you don't make any further comments."[86] However, one individual who claimed to have attended rainbow parties offered this rejoinder: "[RP24, in response to RP23] Let's see if I have this straight: Since we all know that rainbow parties don't happen, if someone claims to have been to a "rainbow party," that's evidence that they are lying. Thus there is no evidence for rainbow parties. Thus we know that they don't happen. Riiiiiiiight."[87]

Other comments argued that belief or skepticism could be linked to politics and the larger culture wars:

[SB53] the "sex bracelet" is a right-wing urban legend. I don't know what's more laughable: the hysterical puritans who are shocked—SHOCKED!—to discover that preteens have sexual thoughts, or the idea that a middle-aged Post reporters fluent in the "secret code" of fifth grade girls.[88]

[SB54] Snopes is a Leftist site, run by Leftist activists, and aggressively promote a Leftist agenda.[89]

[SB55] None of these articles actually found even a single kid who earnest claimed to have done this. Yeah, the breathless reporting actually tends to be done by fundie authors who want everyone to believe that teens and preteens are being turned into mindless sex zombies because they haven't welcomed Jebus into their lives.[90]

Relocating the Activity

Believers sought to argue that rainbow parties and sex bracelets were real sexual practices, even as most of them denied that they had direct involvement with these practices. One way to make this argument was to suggest that it was other people—different sorts of people—who were directly involved. Because much of the attention to these stories derived from the claims that these were common practices among people who were surprisingly young, many comments suggested that rainbow parties and sex bracelets were indeed common; it was just that they occurred among somewhat older people:

> [RP25] Ah, yes the days of the rainbow parties. I was like in the fifth grade when i statred hearing about it (the eighth graders were doing naughty things! jk).[91]

> [SB56] I'm in 7th grade in middle school ! And people play this game called "Snap" when you snap the bracelet you have to do what it means . But , the kids do it for fun . They don't actually do it . Now , older kids (high schoolers) probably do .[92]

> [SB57] It is college students and twentysomethings who actually ascribe sexual meaning to these bracelets.[93]

[SB58] These bracelets wouldnt have even exisited if it wasnt for some adults who had made a game called snap.[94]

Other comments relocated these practices to particular sorts of people or particular places:

[SB59] Im 13 and I have a lot of those bracelets but in my school we dont think of them like that . Some 'nasty' kids may use them like that because they're trying to grow up too fast.[95]

[SB60] They may be used for them in other towns, but in my town, certainly not. So really, it depends on the town.[96]

[RP26] Rainbow party: The thing that causes an outbreak of herpes among the freshman class at [name of school].[97]

In addition to the different color keys for sex bracelets, the stories about the sexual practices involved in rainbow parties and sex bracelets varied among the various online comments. It was unclear, for instance, whether a shag band had to be snapped, broken, or pulled off or whether the colors denoted acts already performed or acts the wearer was willing to perform. And there were still other variants:

[SB61] The version I was told had nothing to do with some silly game, they were more like charm bracelets. Each color stood for a different good thing that could happen to a person (or a different sexual act) and when the bracelet snapped off of its own accord, that good thing was supposed to happen to the person. Obviously, in all cases, black means 'sex' so in the version I learned if you were wearing a black bracelet, and it broke off one day; you were going to have sex soon.[98]

[SB62] I've heard they mean sex stuff but only when you twist them together.[99]

[SB63] The main idea is if they break u have to do the thing they represent, to the person who gave u them or who broke it, or in some cases the nearest to you at the time.[100]

Similarly, comments could not agree on the rules that governed rainbow parties. Some portrayed it as a competition, although they might not agree on the nature of the contest:

[RP27] The guy with the most the color on his dick wins.[101]

[RP28] The girl with her lipstick farthest down on the most boys is deemed "winner."[102]

Parental Fears, Rape, and Other Adult Issues

Skeptics sometimes argued that concerns about rainbow parties and sex bracelets were rooted in overwrought adult anxieties:

[SB64] I think part of the driving force for these panics are a parents fear of their children's pre-sexual behavior. They are uncomfortable with games like doctor or kisschase, or spin the bottle or any of these games children often play as a way to explore their beginning sexuality. And really, in a society that is also panicked by the thought of molestation or sexualization of children, they really have no tools to handle this. When you are so hung up on "sex between children and adults/older children is wrong" it is hard to see that maybe this innocent exploration between peers is not wrong.[103]

[RP29] Excuse my French but adults who believe this sort of stuff is dumb beyond measure.[104]

[SB65] Hysterical adults on one side and pedo dreamers with wild fantasies of delusion on the other.[105]

[SB66] That's what we expect from school administrators—knee-JERK reactions based entirely upon RUMORS! Idiots!![106]

On the other hand, believers pointed to the possibility that kids' sexual play might lead to rape or other terrible consequences:

[SB67] The colors and styles re not the same everywhere which poses a problem. A kid from one place thinks they are sending a signal in one form that means something else in another place or to another person.[107]

[SB68] It DOES allow a point of access for predatory adults to use in order to begin the process of grooming and manipulation.[108]

[SB69] I am a school resource officer and we have made our kids stop wearing them. . . . You teens think its all funny until the wrong person breaks it and wants to cash in on there prize, then what you refuse to do it and they take matters into their own hands, then we have a lil girl or boy sreaming rape because they think it is cool to wear them.[109]

These scenarios also appear in rape tales told in comments:

[SB70] They shud just ban them coz FUCKING 7 YEAR OLD KIDS ARE GETN RAPED BCOZ OF THEM DICKHEAD, THTS WAT U DON'T FUCKING UNDERSTAND.[110]

[SB71] An 8 year old was walkin bk from skool and a man grabbed the shag band snapped it and broke it than toke this 8 year old in the bush and rapped her that is why i will now where thm.[111]

In this debate, believers argued that sexual play posed dangers too great to be ignored. One said, "[SB72] a parent can never be over protective nowadays."[112] But skeptics insisted that the risks of rainbow parties and sex bracelets had been blown far out of proportion.

Arguing over Reports of Teen Sex

Too often, we think of public opinion in terms of polls. When done well, surveys have advantages: they draw large, representative samples of the national population; and they can measure the relative frequency of different responses to particular questions. At the same time, survey research is expensive, and the number of questions asked is limited, so that complex attitudes tend to be distilled into forced responses to a single question—for which candidate do you plan to vote? do you favor or oppose some proposed law? and so on.

The Internet allows us to approach public opinion from a different angle. Online postings are not produced by a statistically representative sample of the population, but they do offer a more nuanced sense of the sorts of thing people are saying. This chapter has examined the range of comments posted on blogs and discussion threads about sex bracelets and rainbow parties, and it is clear that there was a great diversity in people's reactions to these stories.

In order to bring some order to the confusion, we have classified the people making comments into believers (who basically accepted the notion that some young people were engaging in sexual behavior through rainbow parties or sex bracelets) and skeptics (who doubted that these practices were all that common or serious). This is not how people identified themselves; it is our own analytic distinction—a way of helping to make sense of what people said. We have further classified comments by the sorts of evidence or arguments they presented. Table 4.1 summarizes what we found.

It is important to appreciate that well over half the comments in our sample do not fit any of the categories represented in table 4.1. In particular, hundreds of comments about sex bracelets—many by young people—ignored the debate; their posts spoke to how many bracelets they had, which colors were their favorites, how bracelets functioned as fashion, or what particular colors meant. Similarly, discussion threads with adult participants often drifted away from their initial focus on

Table 4.1. Basic Online Arguments about Rainbow Parties (RP) or Sex Bracelets (SB) Made by Believers and Skeptics

Type of evidence	Believers	Skeptics
Firsthand accounts	I've participated in RP or SB.	My experiences do not support the stories.
Secondhand reports	I know people who've participated.	The people I know haven't participated.
Role of media	Media reports confirm the stories.	Media reports cannot be trusted.
Role of business (SB)	Business promotes SB.	Business doesn't promote SB.
Importance of social change	Social change causes RP or SB.	These stories resemble earlier tales; any changes are illusionary.
Assessing plausibility	These stories are plausible.	These stories are not plausible.
Need for evidence (RP)		There should be better evidence of RP.
Relocating activity	These stories apply to other people.	
Variants	RP and SB take different forms	
Adult fears	RP and SB are extremely dangerous.	Fears of RP and SB are overblown.

rainbow parties or sex bracelets into more general comments about parenting practices, schools, politics, religion's dwindling influence, the general moral climate, and so on. We did not try to code all of the comments and present quantitative data, simply because the residual category would have been so large.

Rather, our goal is to show that discussions of contemporary legends are complex; people are more than passive recipients of these stories. Some people had no trouble believing reports about rainbow parties and sex bracelets, but others dismissed them out of hand. Both believers and skeptics advanced different sorts of evidence and developed different lines of reasoning to support their positions, and table 4.1 summarizes the way we've classified their arguments. Note that the two positions tended to adopt parallel claims—they made use of the same sorts of reasoning. This reflects the common cultural assumptions of believers and skeptics. Thus, both accepted that first-person accounts might offer relevant evidence, so that some believers said that they had personal experience with either rainbow parties or sex bracelets, just as some skeptics recounted their own experiences as evidence that the stories were not accurate portrayals of kids' sexual behaviors. Logically, of course, a believer's firsthand account is more powerful. Comments in which individuals reported having attended rainbow parties (see RP1 and RP3) suggested that such parties did in fact occur, whereas someone saying he or she personally has never participated in a rainbow party is hardly proof that such parties don't take place. This is why some skeptics challenged the authenticity of firsthand accounts of attending rainbow parties (see RP4 and RP23), but no one bothered to cast doubt on firsthand skeptical reports.

Similarly, both believers and skeptics offered secondhand reports, discussed the media's role in spreading the stories, and so on. Table 4.1 reminds us that believers and skeptics adopted parallel rhetorical techniques; they presented the analogous sorts of evidence and reasoning. The table also demonstrates that, for the most part, the debates about rainbow parties and sex bracelets paralleled each other. There were a couple of exceptions: the sex-bracelet debate featured speculation about whether the businesses that manufactured the bracelets were knowingly corrupting their young customers (whereas there were no parallel comments questioning whether lipstick manufacturers ought to be implicated in rainbow parties); and skeptics questioned whether there was enough evidence to support claims for the existence of rainbow parties (whereas the fact that lots of young people were visibly wearing sex bracelets did not allow a parallel skeptical argument). But, for the most part, the two debates occurred along parallel lines.

For believers, the underlying theme was that today's kids have more sexual knowledge and are engaging in a broader array of sexual practices, and at earlier ages, than in the past. Contemporary legends often impart a conservative message; they warn that the world has is becoming less moral and more dangerous. Claims about rainbow parties and sex bracelets portrayed young people as increasingly engaging in sexual activities that are governed by a set of impersonal rules that are divorced from love, intimacy, or even caring. That is, the very idea of a rainbow party implied that there could be some agreement among various girls to coordinate lipstick colors and then fellate at least one boy; this envisioned oral sex as having become a public, calculated activity. Similarly, the shag-band story required that kids share an understanding of the sexual meanings of different bracelet colors, as well as being ready to perform the various acts with whoever qualified by snapping—or removing or breaking—a bracelet. Both stories imagined young people as willingly engaging in sexual acts simply because they were following a set of rules for sexual play. The stories were vague and invited questions that, in turn, led to embellished tales about just these things (see RP25–26 and SB56–60) or about terrible consequences when things went wrong (see SB70–71). For believers, these stories were troubling because they depicted young people who are no longer guided by traditional values.

Skeptics, in contrast, redefined the problem as the stories themselves. While they conceded the impossibility of demonstrating that rainbow parties never had and never would happen or that sex bracelets never had and never would lead to troubling sexual practices, they considered the tales unlikely and believers as credulous. Just as believers envisioned a society experiencing moral decay, skeptics offered social criticism: they charged the media with uncritically spreading unreliable claims (see RP13 and SB18–22) and believers with giving in to excessive fears (RP29 and SB64–66). More importantly, they drew on their personal experiences, recalling their own sexual play and reinterpreting stories about rainbow parties and sex bracelets as simply the latest versions of much older tales.

We have classified rainbow parties and sex bracelets as contemporary legends not because we are claiming that these tales are simply false but because the evidence supporting these stories is so thin. Chapter 3 explored how television programs—ranging from news shows to talk shows and other sorts of infotainment to fictional dramatic programs—relayed these stories without subjecting them to much critical assessment. This chapter has shown that, in contrast, the Internet provided a forum where people could debate the meaning of these reports of rainbow parties and sex bracelets. Believers found the stories credible and sought to explain why they considered rainbow parties and sex bracelets phenomena that deserved public attention and concern, even as skeptics expressed doubts and tried to account for their reservations.

Chapter 5 turns to the teen sexting crisis. An examination of the media's coverage of teen sexting reveals that unlike the sex-bracelet and rainbow-party tales, the phenomenon of teens sending and receiving sexual text messages and images via cell phones was well documented. However, the media's portrayal of sexting was very similar in that much of the coverage was overblown. A closer look at sexting also illustrates how exaggerated claims about today's teens has led to more than simply justifying or heightening fear among parents and other adults—it has prompted many attempts to control behavior (in this case, to curb sexting). Ultimately, we will argue that the hype over teen sex has given people a distorted view of youthful sexual behavior, thereby unduly affecting people's decisions on how to respond.

5

Controlling Teen Sexting

Sexting is so rampant that we would cripple the criminal
court system if we could actually pursue everyone.
—B. J. Bernstein, on *Tell Me More* (NPR), 2011

The contemporary legends about sex bracelets and rainbow parties
were propelled by fear—worries about today's kids engaging in sexual
behavior too soon and being exposed to sex at ever younger ages. There
is a cycle here: the media capitalizes on these fears by running sensational stories about teen sex; these stories in turn fuel the public's fear;
and this makes the topic even more attractive for media coverage. But
the cycle is not restricted to the media and public opinion. The concerns people have about sex and today's kids manifest themselves in
more ways than media coverage and personal angst. As much as people
express their concern by *talking* about teens and sex—whether in media
coverage or in conversations at home, in schools, or online—there are
also efforts to take action, to *do* something, to control sexual behavior
among the young.

Of course, this is nothing new. Most societies devise ways to control the sexual behavior of youth. These efforts have a long history; for
instance, in the United States in recent decades, there has been a debate
about the appropriate role of the public schools in educating students
about sexuality.[1] Some people favor a comprehensive sex-education

approach. Advocates of this position, the *sexual liberals* who adopt what we characterized in chapter 1 as a pragmatic position, tend to favor including information on sexually transmitted diseases, condoms, and abortion in the curriculum. Sexual liberals take teen sexual activity as a given and seek to implement a harm-reduction approach by reducing unwanted pregnancies and sexually transmitted diseases. Since they do not object to teens having sex per se, sexual liberals' focus is on teaching teens how to have "safe sex." On the other side of the debate are the *sexual conservatives*, described in chapter 1 as advocating a protective position, who in recent years have rallied around the slogan "abstinence only." They believe that teaching about safe sex actually condones or promotes teen sex, whereas they believe that sexual intercourse should be postponed until the individual matures and enters into marriage. Furthermore, sexual conservatives argue that because no contraceptive method is 100% effective, the concept of safe sex is grossly misleading and may make teens believe they are safer than they actually are. As a result, sexual conservatives believe teens must be taught that abstinence is the only safe—and morally correct—way to behave while waiting to enter into marriage.[2]

Even as the battle over sex education continues, parallel debates have emerged over other issues. Social changes often have ramifications for teen sexuality, so that developments in popular culture, fashion, and technology can lead to calls for new controls on teens. In recent years, the wide availability of cellular phones and the capability of text messaging produced the teen sexting controversy. The tumult over sexting illustrates how society's concern over teen sex inspires debates over the best ways to curtail kids' sexual behavior.

The Emergence of Sexting

The teen sexting problem began to draw attention in the United States in 2008, when some local newspapers and local television news programs around the country started running stories about teens having been caught with sexual pictures of one another on their cellular phones.[3] After papers such as the *Salt Lake Tribune* began covering the topic ("Authorities Alarmed by Trends of Teens Sending and Receiving Nude Photos via Cell Phone"), the Associated Press picked up the story in June:

> Passing notes in study hall or getting your best friend to ask a boy if he likes you or, you know, LIKES you, is so last century. Nowadays, teenagers are snapping naked pictures of themselves on their cell phones and sending them to their boyfriends and girlfriends. Many of these pictures are falling into the wrong hands or worse, everyone's hands, via the Internet and leading to criminal charges. Some parents are aghast.[4]

The AP story highlighted several cases around the country of teens being punished for sending or receiving sexual images of themselves or classmates. It contained quotes from parents, psychologists, and police, each attempting to explain why teens were engaging in this new and troubling behavior.

Later that summer, the AP ran another story on sexting, reporting that a 16-year-old boy from Utah had been sentenced for sending pictures of his abdomen and groin to a classmate he was dating. According to the article, the boy also asked the girl to send him a naked picture in return. When she sought help from school officials, it led to the boy being charged with three felonies. Ultimately, "the teen pleaded guilty to a pair of class A misdemeanor charges of dealing in harmful material to a minor."[5]

Several similar stories received media coverage during 2008, but the topic of sexting—and the term—picked up steam in December, when CosmoGirl.com and the National Campaign to Prevent Teen and Unplanned Pregnancy released the results of a survey of over 1,000 teens and young adults about their use of technology to engage in flirtatious banter or to send and receive sexual images of one another. *USA Today* reported the results under the headline "In Tech Flirting, Decorum Optional: Racy Pics, Messages Flying among Young": "Passing a flirtatious note to get someone's attention is so yesterday. These days, young people use technology instead. About a third of young adults 20–26 and 20% of teens say they've sent or posted naked or semi-naked photos or videos of themselves, mostly to be 'fun or flirtatious,' a survey finds."[6] The article reported that 39% of teens had sent a sexually suggestive text (written) message and that one-quarter of teen girls and one-third of teen boys had seen nude or seminude images of a classmate that were initially sent to someone else.[7]

The survey's results inspired a wave of coverage by both newspapers and television news programs. While previous stories had reported on isolated incidents, from this point forward the media declared that there was a *widespread* sexting problem among teens, so that particular cases could now be understood as instances of a larger phenomenon. In addition to claiming that sexting was widespread, the media warned that sexting could lead to serious consequences for teens. Consider how NBC's *Today Show* cohosts Meredith Vieira and Matt Lauer framed the topic:

> VIEIRA: And then a really disturbing story for parents. You might call this "sexting," teens sending nude or seminude pictures of themselves on their cell phones or online. A staggering number are doing it. One out of five teenage girls say they are; almost as many boys. We're going to talk about why they do it and the repercussions, a real warning for parents out there.
>
> LAUER: They may not think it has repercussions now in the short term.
>
> VIEIRA: But it does.
>
> LAUER: But this could affect them long down the road.

Vieira then spoke with two experts, Marisa Nightingale from the National Campaign to Prevent Teen and Unplanned Pregnancy and Susan

Schulz from *CosmoGirl* magazine, about the results of their study and its implications.

> VIEIRA: What do teens not understand about the possible repercussions of putting these pictures out there?
>
> NIGHTINGALE: I think they don't understand that these things really never die. Nothing in cyberspace ever really goes away, and something done on a whim or even on a dare can haunt you for the rest of your life, when you're looking for a job, when you're applying for a college scholarship, so . . .
>
> SCHULZ: Colleges regularly look at profiles now just . . . because they want to see, well, what kind of kid is this. On paper, you know, star soccer player, community service, straight-A student. . . . But what are they doing in their social time?[8]

Three days later, ABC's *World News Tonight* covered sexting. It, too, characterized the practice as widespread among teens and warned that it might be happening among "some children as young as the fourth grade." In addition to warning that sexted images can spread "like wild-fire," ABC News correspondent Gigi Stone also cautioned teens and their parents about sexting's potential criminal ramifications:

> The consequences can go beyond embarrassment. Around the country, teens are being prosecuted as sex offenders. This year in Wisconsin, a 17-year-old was charged with possessing child pornography after he posted naked pictures of his 16-year-old ex-girlfriend. In Alabama, authorities arrested four middle school students for exchanging nude photos. In Rochester, New York, a 16-year-old boy is now facing up to seven years in prison for forwarding a nude photo of a girlfriend to his friends.[9]

In January 2009, CBS's *Early Show* joined the other networks in sounding the alarm about teen sexting. Interviews with a police officer and a legal analyst emphasized the seriousness of the problem.

HARRY SMITH (COHOST): Six teenagers . . . in Greensburg, Pennsylvania, are learning an even harder lesson this week. Three girls allegedly sent nude photos to three teenage boys, and all six now face charges of child pornography. . . . For now, the investigation in Pennsylvania continues, and police say more charges could be filed.

CAPTAIN GEORGE SERANKO (GREENSBURG POLICE): It's very dangerous, and it could come back and harm not only the victim that took the picture but their families.

SMITH: We're joined by Lisa Bloom, CBS News legal analyst. . . . What do you think of this?

BLOOM: Well, technically they are violating the letter of the law. Anyone who distributes or possesses child pornography, naked pictures of underage kids . . . is looking at child porn charges. By the way, this is a serious felony. They could be facing many years in prison. They could have to register as sex offenders . . . for the rest of their lives.

SMITH: It says one in five kids are doing this sort of thing.

BLOOM: Right. So what are we going to do? Lock up 20% of America's teenagers?[10]

As concern about sexting mounted, some advocates argued that making teens aware of the criminal penalties was the answer to the problem. Also that January, *The Today Show* aired another segment on sexting, this time featuring an expert on Internet safety:

PARRY AFTAB (EXECUTIVE DIRECTOR, WIREDSAFETY.ORG): The sexual images of underage kids is child pornography. And until recently, law enforcement was just not getting involved. Now they are.

KATHIE LEE GIFFORD (COANCHOR): Why are they now? What's changed?

AFTAB: They are so frustrated. We've got these kids posing in the nude when they're not old enough to wear bras.[11]

The initial reports on sexting focused on the discovery that kids were using new cell phone technology and other social media devices, such as Facebook, to send and receive sexually explicit photos and messages presented adults with a dilemma. While some might have deemed sexting a minor matter, just another way for kids to enjoy sexual play, others considered it a serious matter, worthy of concern. The most extreme reaction was to treat sexting as a serious crime; this could lead to youths receiving harsh penalties. As more incidents were reported and the survey data on sexting was released, the national media picked up the story and chose to frame sexting as both a widespread trend and a serious matter worthy of grave concern. The media's coverage emphasized the dire consequences that teens faced if they were caught sexting and the importance of making sure all kids were aware of those consequences. Given the extent of the media coverage, most people were now aware of claims about sexting, although debate continued over the best way to handle it.

The Sexting Debate

Reports of child pornography charges being applied in teen sexting cases launched a debate about whether this was the best approach. As early as February 2009, numerous experts and other commentators weighed in on sexting; they called for lesser penalties or, in some cases, decriminalizing it altogether. For example, the *St. Petersburg Times* quoted a psychologist: "Sexting is not a matter for the courts unless it's done with malicious intent, such as kids taking photos without permission or forwarding them spitefully."[12] *Newsweek* posed this question: "Ask yourself: should the police be involved when tipsy teen girls email their boyfriends naughty Valentine's Day pictures?":

> One quick clue that the criminal justice system is probably not the best venue for addressing the sexting crisis? A survey of the charges brought in the cases reflects that—depending on jurisdiction—prosecutors have charged the senders of smutty photos, the recipients of smutty photos, those who save the smutty photos, and the hapless forwarders of smutty

photos with the same crime: child pornography. Who is the victim here and who is the perpetrator? Everybody and nobody.

The article acknowledged that, while it might be appropriate to impose criminal penalties in cases of sexting that also involved *cyberbullying*, "the criminal justice system is too blunt an instrument to resolve a problem that reflects more about the volatile combination of teens and technology than some national cyber-crime spree."[13]

Reports soon followed that law enforcement officials themselves were questioning the criminal justice system's handling of sexting cases: "Ohio prosecutors and others are pressing lawmakers to update pornography . . . laws to better apply to teenagers. The move comes as prosecutors debate what to do about teens who send racy images on cell phones. Law enforcement officials want to deter teenagers but believe current penalties under Ohio's child pornography laws are too harsh."[14]

While the controversy surrounding how to address sexting from a legal standpoint continued, alternative ways to combat the problem surfaced. A *Good Morning America* segment on how to prevent teens from misusing cell phones, including sexting and texting while driving, recommended that parents fight technology with technology.

> BECKY WORLEY (ABC CORRESPONDENT): Cell phone carriers do offer some parental controls, blocking numbers and limiting usage. But now, new software called Web Safety lets worried parents all but take over their teen's phone. . . . The software alerts parents whenever their kids use sexually explicit or suggestive language, including words like *meet up* or *hook up*. The Web Safety software costs $99 for the year. . . . Bottom line, parents want more control of their kids' cell phones. . . . And they'll do anything to get that control.
>
> DAVID MUIR (COANCHOR): It sounds so much like Big Brother. But a lot of teens don't realize that the pictures and the texts that they send out, especially those salacious photos, can come back to haunt you when you apply for a job and for college.

WORLEY: The ramifications are very serious. And while there is a technology solution with this type of software, it's an awareness issue for parents. Parents need to be in the know that this is what their kids are
doing, so they can talk to them before they get into trouble.[15]

This exchange illustrates our culture's ambivalence toward technology. New technologies bring advantages, but they often inspire concerns about their effects on children, such as concerns that the Internet exposes kids to pornography, sexual predators, and cyberbullying.
Because most people consider technology's advantages to outweigh its
risks, there is little enthusiasm for banning it. Instead, there are efforts
to manage the technology, as in offering software to track cell phone use.

While some people favored enhancing parental control of teens
through more sophisticated technology, others suggested that schools
should play an active role in preventing teen sexting. CNN's *Newsroom*
reported on one school district's sexting policy:

A school district in southwest Washington is upping the ante against students sexting, and they're not playing around. The Kelso School District
voted, unanimously, this week, to ban all explicit messages sent from students' phones on school property. That includes any sexual pictures, text
messages, and e-mails that students send. So how will school officials
know? Well, get this. Under the new code, school administrators will be
allowed to confiscate and search students' personal cell phones. If a student is caught sexting, parents and police are notified. A second or third
offense, that's a long-term suspension and even expulsion. The district's
ban on sexting goes into effect this fall.[16]

Both parental-control software and new school policies were designed to allow adults to control teens and thereby reduce sexting; however, some people called for a different approach, one that would reduce
the problem by educating teens themselves about the dangers of sexting.
Beginning in 2009, several antisexting campaigns were launched. One

prominent campaign was MTV's "A Thin Line," which was designed to combat sexting and related issues, such as "cyberbullying" or "textual harassment." The MTV campaign was designed to talk directly to teens and get them to think twice about their actions. The website devoted to this campaign posed the following questions:

> *Was this my idea?* If you're not in the mood to make, take, or share a permanent record of your stuff, choose a way to express your hotness that won't put you at risk for major overexposure. If you're being pressured to pose, and feel embarrassed to say no, play along, but keep your clothes on—*not* showing it all is way sexier. Still on the fence? Proceed to part two of this question: is it better to feel uncool for a half an hour or be totally humiliated when the pics wind up in everybody's inbox?
>
> *Where will this picture end up? Possible answers:* a) My bf or gf's phone. b) His or her friends' phones. c) Everyone's phone and inbox.

The website also listed what could happen if teens choose to sext: you could gain a bad reputation if the sext gets forwarded or risk a future relationship because your prospective mate will assume "you send naked pictures of yourself to everyone" and reject you as a result. Finally, the site warned of the possibility of criminal penalties: "*What could happen?* You get arrested. Taking, sending, and possessing naked images of a minor is a federal crime. Sex offenders' registry? Not the honor roll you were hoping for."[17]

Although the MTV campaign was written with gender-neutral language, the underlying message seemed to be warning *girls* not to give in to pressure to send sexual pictures of themselves. Several other groups launched their own antisexting campaigns, which more often than not focused on warnings to girls. The United Way produced an ad which pictured a cell phone covered in a condom with the caption, "Practice Safe Text."[18] An article in the *Wall Street Journal* highlighted other campaigns by the Ad Council, the Family Violence Prevention Fund, and Common Sense Media. The Ad Council used television to get across

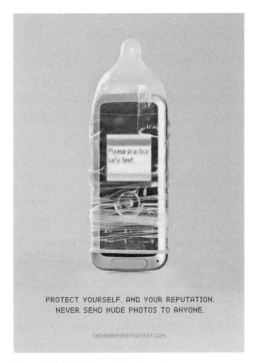

Fig. 5.1. United Way antisexting ad

its message through a series of public-service announcements, which included the slogan, "Think before you post."

> One [ad] depicts a teenage girl who keeps getting creepy comments from people who seem to know intimate things about her. The football coach compliments her on her new tattoo. The ticket collector at the movie theater asks what color underwear she's wearing today. Then we hear a voice saying "anything you post online, anyone can see." Another video shows a girl posting a picture on a bulletin board that instantly reappears after someone takes it down, allowing everyone at the school—even the janitor—to get a copy.[19]

The media reports indicated that people were not just worrying about teen sexting; they were *doing* a host of things to try to control it.

Initially, teens who were caught sexting were being punished through the criminal justice system. Police were making arrests, and prosecutors were pursuing cases. Since there were no laws specifically designed to address sexting per se, some prosecutors decided to apply child pornography laws that were already on the books. These laws generally carry harsh sentences and lifelong ramifications for those who are convicted, including being labeled a felon and having to register as a sex offender. While some people favored applying existing child pornography laws to sexting cases (and using the threat of these harsh penalties as a deterrent), others insisted that this approach was too severe. Those against applying child pornography laws to sexting argued that these laws were meant to punish adult child molesters, not teens exchanging sexual images. As a result, in some states, lawmakers began drafting proposals for sexting-specific legislation that would lessen the penalty for sexting offenses.

Other attempts to control sexting focused on limiting kids' ability to access the technology. In some cases, this meant changes in school policies, such as banning sexting on school grounds and rules allowing cell phones to be confiscated and searched. Access could also be stifled by software designed to allow parents oversight of the contents of their children's phones.

Still others deemed education the best way to tackle the sexting problem. Advocates developed public-service announcements and other campaigns to raise awareness among young people about the dangers of sexting. Thus, although there was no consensus on the best way to stop teens from sexting, it seemed that many people agreed it was a serious problem and that something ought to be done about it.

The Media Run with the Story

At first glance, the media's coverage of sexting was not that different from the way it framed sex bracelets and rainbow parties; all three stories featured warnings to parents that teens were out of control, a danger to themselves, and that something needed be done to stop them. But there were important differences. First, as noted in chapter 2, sexting was receiving far more coverage than either of the other stories were. Moreover, sexting stories could be illustrated with specific incidents. It is common for the news to cover trends, that is, to portray topics as increasingly visible and important phenomena, and there were examples of stories describing shag bands, rainbow parties, and sexting as trends. But coverage of sex bracelets and rainbow parties consisted almost exclusively of this sort of trend talk; yet, although people might insist that some kids, somewhere, were following the sex-bracelet/rainbow-party rules for sexual play, there wasn't much in the way of hard evidence. And, as we have suggested, this ambiguity, this absence of evidence, is characteristic of contemporary legends.

In contrast, the news was filled with stories of particular sexting incidents: a boy in this school had sent sexual messages to a girl, and she had complained; while in that school, a girl had sent a sexual picture to her boyfriend, and the images had spread throughout the school; at yet another school, sexting had led to a teen girl committing suicide; in still another community, kids had been arrested, even convicted, on criminal charges. And of course there was that survey suggesting that lots of kids had been involved in sexting, either sending or receiving—or at least viewing—sexual texts and images. In other words, talk about sexting went beyond claims that it was a trend. The issue required something beyond the sort of "be responsible and talk to your teen" parenting promoted by the talk shows.

However, like most teen-sex stories, the media's coverage of sexting capitalized on people's fears by highlighting the most extreme cases and thereby presented their audience a distorted view of the issue. There were three cases, all of which received considerable media attention, that were used in reports as *typifying examples* to illustrate the sexting problem. Such "typifying examples are, in fact, rarely typical. Usually they are chosen to illustrate the seriousness of the problem, so they tend to be especially extreme, dramatic, disturbing, memorable cases."[20]

The first case occurred in Wyoming County, Pennsylvania. School officials at Tunkhannock high school discovered that boys at the school were trading nude and seminude images of female classmates, which initially had been sent voluntarily by the girls, and turned the case over to the district attorney's office for investigation. The district attorney assigned to the case sent a letter to 20 parents informing them that their children were involved in a potential child pornography case and that he would pursue "felony child pornography charges" unless the students who appeared in the photos or were found to possess the photos submitted to an education program. The five-week education program cost $100 and included information designed to "gain an understanding of what it means to be a girl in today's society." The students in question would also be put on probation and be subject to random drug testing.[21]

Most parents agreed to the education program to avoid their child getting charged with a felony, but the parents of three of the girls accused of appearing in pornographic photos contacted the American Civil Liberties Union and filed suit against the district attorney, arguing that the pictures were not child pornography and that the DA was abusing his power by threatening to charge them under child pornography laws. In the first of the two pictures in question, two of the teen girls (who were 12 when the photo was taken) appeared in opaque, white bras. One girl was talking on the phone and the other was giving the peace sign. In a second picture, one girl appeared topless with a towel around her waist. The ACLU won the case on behalf of the girls and their parents when the Third Circuit Court of Appeals decided that the prosecutor could not charge the girls for appearing in the photos. This story was highlighted in the news over a two-year period from the time the pictures began circulating until the appeal was won. Media coverage of the case reinforced the notion that very young girls were engaged in lewd behavior (as two of the girls in this case were not even teenagers at the time the photo was taken). It also reinforced that kids could face harsh legal consequences if caught sexting.

The second case that dominated headlines involved a female high

school senior from Ohio who sexted a nude photo of herself to her boyfriend; he then forwarded the photo to others upon the breakup of their
relationship. She was relentlessly teased and harassed by those who had
seen the photo. The school she attended was aware of the situation, but
nothing could be done from a legal standpoint because she was already
18 and so the photo of her could not be classified as child pornography.
The summer after graduation, her mother found that she had hanged
herself in her bedroom with her cell phone in the middle of the floor.
After the tragedy, her mother gave interviews to the press in an effort to
educate the public about the dangers of sexting.[22]

The third typifying example came from Orlando, Florida. An 18-
year-old, male high school senior had naked photos of his 16-year-old
girlfriend that she had previously sexted him. One night, after an argument, he decided to forward those photos to everyone in his girlfriend's
email contact list. He was charged with 72 offenses, including possessing and distributing child pornography, and he was sentenced to five
years probation and added to the national sex-offender registry until
age 43.[23]

The latter two cases served as the ultimate examples of why the
media suggested that parents needed to be warned of the dangers of
sexting. The media used them for dramatic effect to show parents how
sexting could lead to worst-case scenarios: if your daughter sexts, she
could be humiliated to the point of taking her own life; and if your son
sexts, he could be labeled a child pornographer and have to register as
a sex offender. Although most incidents of teen sexting did not have
such horrific and irreversible results, these cases were often presented
accompanied by data indicating sexting's prevalence (most often claims
that 20% of American teens were sexting).[24] However, some members
of the media went further, suggesting that 20% was a low estimate or
that "all" teens were sexting. For example, amid a discussion of the Florida case cited earlier, CBS News legal analyst Jack Ford offered this on
the prevalence of sexting: "And we're hearing that something like 20%
of kids have admitted to doing this. So that percentage is admitting it.

How many others are out there doing it and not admitting it?"[25] After discussing the suicide in Ohio that had been linked to sexting, CNN's Drew Pinsky stated, "And most all of [teens] agree [sexting] is not such a good thing, and most all of them agree *they're all doing it*."[26]

In addition to claims that sexting was widespread, many media reports emphasized that very young children were involved, especially young girls. While some media accounts portrayed girls as innocent victims who needed to be protected from the dangers of sexting, other accounts focused on girls as the initiators of sexting. These stories suggested that girls today are more brazen than girls in previous eras were. An episode of CNN's *American Morning* covered all three cases cited earlier. As others had done, reporter Deborah Feyerick referred to the pervasiveness of sexting by calling it a "fast growing trend" among teens that "one in five say they've done." Then, Feyerick and anchor Carol Costello had this discussion to point out how young girls are involved:

> FEYERICK: And the funny thing is its girls who are sending these pictures to boys, young girls.
>
> COSTELLO: And that's what's so dumbfounding. I'm floored with how comfortable they must be with their bodies at age 12. I mean, I wanted to hide myself. Like, what's going on there?[27]

Coupling the most extreme examples to statistics indicating that sexting was widespread among young teens was a recipe for a compelling media story, but it was misleading. Claims of sexting being an "epidemic" among teens and preteens were based on a combination of anecdotal evidence and the *CosmoGirl* survey, released in December 2008. Like many such magazine-sponsored surveys, this poll was not based on a random sample, so that most social scientists would not consider the information reliable. Rather, the survey was conducted online using those who volunteered to participate—that is, a convenience sample—and therefore the results should not have been generalized to all teens in the U.S. Furthermore, the oft-cited statistic from the survey that 20%

of teens had sent or posted nude or seminude pictures of themselves
was based on responses from 13- to 19-year-olds. Using this statistic to
generalize about all kids is problematic for two reasons: (a) the sample
does not include preteens at all, so there can be no conclusions drawn
for this group, and (b) it combines 18- and 19-year-old adults (for whom
sexting is not illegal) with other teens who are still minors.

By contrast, a second study, released in December 2009 by the Pew
Research Center and American Life Project and carried out by Princeton Survey Research, found a much lower proportion of teens sexting:
"4% of cell-owning teens ages 12–17 say they have sent sexually suggestive nude or nearly nude images or videos of themselves to someone
else via text messaging, a practice also known as 'sexting.'"[28] The study
also differentiated among cases of sexting and found that the most
common scenario for sexting was that of one teen sending a sexually
provocative self-image to his or her boyfriend or girlfriend. Additionally, in spite of media claims that sexting was a major problem among
kids "as young as the fourth grade," the Pew study found that sexting
was much more common among older teens than younger teens or preteens. This survey was based on a probability sample in three American cities, and participants answered survey questions over the phone.
Unlike the *CosmoGirl* study, those surveyed by Pew were all minors, so
child pornography laws could potentially apply to them for engaging in
sexting. Given that the researchers at Pew focused on minors and their
study was representative, the Pew findings offered a better measure of
how widespread the sexting problem was among those under age 18.
When the Pew study was released, the media did cover it; but by that
time, sexting had already been widely covered using the more provocative *CosmoGirl* data.

Furthermore, as more scholars began examining sexting, questions
were raised about not only whether the sexting phenomenon was as
widespread as the media claimed but also whether cases should be
differentiated from one another instead of being categorized under
one term and handled the same way. Two researchers at the Univer-

sity of New Hampshire's Crimes Against Children Research Center, Janis Wolak and David Finkelhor, analyzed 550 cases of "youth produced sexual images" that occurred in 2008 and 2009, drawn from a national survey of law enforcement agencies. On the basis of their analysis, they divided sexting cases into two major categories: aggravated and experimental:

Aggravated incidents involved criminal or abusive elements beyond the creation, sending or possession of youth-produced sexual images. These additional elements included 1) adult involvement; or 2) criminal or abusive behavior by minors such as sexual abuse, extortion, threats; malicious conduct arising from interpersonal conflicts; or creation or sending or showing of images without the knowledge or against the will of a minor who was pictured. In Experimental incidents, by contrast, youth took pictures of themselves to send to established boy- or girlfriends, to create romantic interest in other youth, or for reasons such as attention-seeking, but there was no criminal behavior beyond the creation or sending of images, no apparent malice and no lack of willing participation by youth who were pictured.[29]

Wolak and Finkelhor came to the sensible conclusion that some forms of sexting, including many of those that fall into the experimental category, ought to be decriminalized, while some of the aggravated incidents should be handled by the criminal justice system.

Thus, upon further examination, the problem of teen sexting was not nearly as dire as the media's portrayal suggested. First, the Pew study raised some doubt about whether sexting was as widespread as originally suggested. Secondly, all cases of sexting are not the same. The most extreme examples of sexting, the stories that made the news, did not accurately reflect what most teens report doing when they admit to sexting. Lastly, the practice of sexting tends to increase with age; in other words, the older people get, the more they sext. Therefore, it is misleading to emphasize sexting's prevalence among very young teens.

Overreaction

Adults who confronted teen sexting found themselves in a tough spot. They had to decide how to respond to this new and troubling phenomenon. But, with the benefit of hindsight, it seems that many went too far. Their overreaction in word and deed likely stemmed from the fervor over teen sex in general. Given the media's exaggerated coverage of teen sex stories, such as sexting, rainbow parties, and sex bracelets, it is reasonable to ask, does media hype influence and distort the national dialogue on teen sex and thereby affect people's decisions on how to respond?

The many actions people took in response to sexting received a great deal of media attention, but sexting was only one of the many stories that have made headlines on the subject of teen sex in recent years. Two other controversies, both involving new pharmaceuticals, were widely covered in the news, and they also call into question how alarmist coverage related to teen-sex hype influences public debates. The first involved Gardasil, a vaccine approved by the FDA in 2006 for females ages 9–26 to protect against cancers caused by sexually transmitted HPV viruses, which if administered before the recipient becomes sexually active, can prevent most cases of cervical cancer.[30] The second concerned Plan B, an emergency contraceptive approved in 1999 that can be taken in pill form by a woman within 72 hours of having unprotected sex.[31]

Initial news coverage treated both drugs as medical breakthroughs, capable of reducing harmful outcomes (cancer and unwanted pregnancy, respectively). But both inspired controversies as sexual liberals pushed the drugs' accessibility for young girls while sexual conservatives argued that making the drugs available might encourage teen sex. For instance, when Texas governor Rick Perry issued an order requiring Gardasil vaccinations for girls entering the sixth grade, critics worried that this would send a message to young girls that they were presumed to be ready for sex.[32] Regardless of which side of the debate one favored, the public discourse on Gardasil reinforced the idea that kids today are having sex at very young ages. Consider this discussion on NPR between host Michel Martin; Dr. Richard Schlegel, the chair of pathology at Georgetown University; and Rebecca Rex, an advocate for vaccine education:

> MARTIN: Why vaccinate at age of 11? I think the recommendation was somewhere between 9 and 11. Why so young? Why not wait until 15 or 16?
>
> SCHLEGEL: Well, if you look at the statistics on when boys and girls become sexually active, that's when it begins. It's the early teens. So if you want to protect someone at the age 13, you better be vaccinating around 11 and 12. And so that's the rationale for beginning at that time period.
>
> MARTIN: What about what [another guest] pointed out, that whether parents like it or not . . . a lot of kids are sexually active at a young age; they think that oral sex isn't sex, and as a consequence of that, perhaps, it really does make sense to offer this additional, I don't know, firewall, if you will. What would you say to that?
>
> REX: Well, I agree with her that we have a lot of parents in denial about the behavior of their children.[33]

Similar tumult surrounded Plan B, which had long encountered opposition for being "abortive" (a claim that scientists disputed), but the real controversy arose in 2011 when the FDA approved making the so-called morning-after pill available to teens without a prescription. When the Obama administration overrode experts' recommendations that Plan B be available over the counter to women under 18 years old, the president explained, "[We] could not be confident that a 10-year-old or an 11-year-old going to a drugstore should be able—alongside bubble gum or batteries—be able to buy a medication that potentially, if not used properly, could have an adverse effect."[34]

Whereas sexual liberals viewed both drugs as harm reducing, sexual conservatives worried that these new medications would promote teens becoming sexually active by reducing some of the risks (cancer, pregnancy) that might deter sex. And as the debate over these policies played out through the press, continual references to sexual activity among very young girls became central to the discussion. Thus, the coverage of these stories continued to support the media's narrative of a teen-sex crisis.

The media's attention to the subject of teen sex provided a platform for a national discussion of the fears people had about kids becoming too sexual too soon. It is possible to look back and recall that adults once thought that youthful passions might be inspired and aroused by close dancing, lipstick, going steady, drive-in movies, rock and roll, short skirts, pierced ears, and the like. These fears have given way to new concerns about the cultural environment that today's kids inhabit, a world that seems filled with Bratz dolls, cable-TV shows that celebrate teen pregnancy, explicit song lyrics, readily accessible online pornography, and on and on. Surely all this stimulation has encouraged more teens to become more sexual. Within this context of concern, stories about rainbow parties, sex bracelets, and pregnancy pacts—tales that might strike many people as unlikely—can seem plausible. If the news reports that a few kids have gotten into serious trouble sexting, surely that's just the tip of the iceberg—a sign of a widespread, serious problem. In this view, teen sexuality becomes a problem so great that sexting teens need to be threatened with felony charges and the sex-offender registry to be kept in check; it is an epidemic so severe that health officials need to make Gardasil and Plan B available to younger and younger girls. Teen sex must be raging out of control—mustn't it?

6

Too Sexual Too Soon

Why Believe the Hype?

From Britney Spears to Abercrombie & Fitch to MTV to sex
bracelets, the sexualization of our youth is everywhere.
—Joe Scarborough on *Scarborough Country*, 2004

Our society seems remarkably worried about young people and sex.
This book has focused on the outrage over sex bracelets, rainbow parties, and sexting, but we have also alluded to other concerns—hooking
up, pregnancy pacts, Gardasil, and Plan B—that flourished at the beginning of the new century. Still other claims got a bit of media attention
(such as the online headline "Group Sex Is the Latest Disturbing Teen
Trend"), only to fade from view.[1] Underpinning the fascination with all
these topics is the fear that today's kids are going wild, that they are sex
obsessed and spiraling out of control. Pop-culture images and media
messages continue to reinforce the impression that kids are having sex
at very young ages and that they are engaging in ever-increasingly promiscuous, reckless sexual behavior.

We've heard the stories, seen the headlines, and watched the pundits rant. Inevitably, they claim that problematic sexual behavior among
teens is common, widespread, and increasing, but they rarely offer much
evidence, beyond an anecdote or two. That is, they don't present much
in the way of data. But there are data available. Precisely because sexual

behavior is risky, in that it can lead to pregnancy, sexually transmitted diseases, or even violence, public health officials conduct research to try and track sexual behavior. In addition, social scientists conduct their own studies. The results of this research reveal patterns in sexual activities, and when we compare the patterns in the data with claims about kids gone wild, it becomes apparent that the fears are overblown.

But this raises another question: if claims about kids gone wild aren't accurate, why are they so widespread? Most of this chapter tries to explain why exaggerated claims—whether in contemporary legends (such as those about shag bands and rainbow parties) or in overblown news stories (such as the coverage of sexting)—flourish. Who believes this stuff, and why?

Questions about Teen Sex: What the Data Show

Discussions of teen sex often assert that "everybody knows" kids are out of control. Our culture—like all cultures—is interested in sex, and we seem to be particularly interested in and worried about sexuality among young people. On the one hand, popular music, movies, and other forms of popular culture celebrate the wonders of young love (which isn't all that new—think of *Romeo and Juliet*). On the other hand, experts encourage us to view teen sex as dangerous: psychologists warn us about the importance of sex in shaping our personalities; doctors describe the medical risks of sexual behavior; politicians worry about the consequences of early pregnancies; while religious authorities focus on the morality of young people's sexual choices.

All these concerns seem more intense because there is a general sense that today's teens are more sexually knowledgeable and experienced than previous generations were. They have easier access to sexual information; the Internet can expose today's children to explicit images of sorts that were far more difficult for members of earlier generations to find. The risks of pregnancy and early parenthood have diminished with easier access to birth control and abortion; thus, some of the consequences that used to deter sexual behavior in previous generations can no longer be counted on to keep teens in check. Who knows what these kids today might be up to? Everybody knows they're out of control; they're getting away with murder.

However, what everybody knows is often quite wrong. Here, we begin with a set of questions: Are today's teens starting to have sex earlier than previous generations did? Are they more promiscuous? And so on. Of course, everybody knows that the answer to each of these questions is yes. And yet researchers who have tried to understand the patterns of sexual behavior among today's young people challenge the conventional wisdom that kids today are out of control.

To be clear, in the discussion that follows, we focus exclusively on research about heterosexual behavior, so that when we refer to sexual intercourse, we mean vaginal intercourse. Virtually all claims about sex bracelets, rainbow parties, and sexting have been framed as concerns about heterosexual behavior (which of course accounts for the great majority of young people's sexual activities), so we contrast those fears with data about heterosexual activity.

Are Today's Teens Having Sex at Much Younger Ages?

> Even 10- and 11-year-olds, they knew how to say, "Homework's done," and then they knew how to have an orgy.
>
> —Michelle Burford on *Oprah*, 2003

Everyone may know that today's kids are becoming sexually active earlier than in the past, but this is one of those cases where everyone is mistaken. Young people today first experience sexual intercourse (on average) at age 17, which is not a drastic change from a generation ago when their parents were coming of age.[2] In fact, the percentage of teens who are sexually active has actually been declining. According to the Centers for Disease Control's National Survey of Family Growth (NSFG), a nationally representative study of teenagers in the United States, the

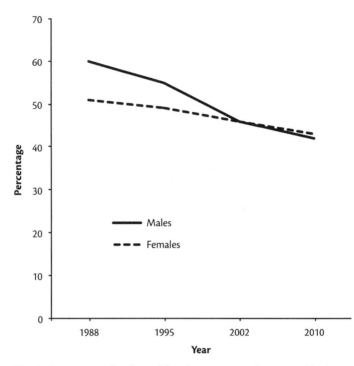

Fig. 6.1. Percentages of males and females ages 15–19 who reported having had sexual intercourse, 1988–2010 (Martinez, Copen, and Abma 2011; data labeled 2010 are for 2006–10).

percentage of young people ages 15–19 who report having had sexual intercourse has significantly decreased over the past 20 years or so. Between 1988 and the latest report (covering 2006–10), the percentage of females who had experienced sex dropped from 51% to 43%, while the comparable percentages for males fell from 60% to 42%.[3] In other words, the majority of teens report that they have never had sex, and the younger the teens, the less likely they are to be sexually experienced.

Data from other studies also demonstrate that the percentage of high school students who are sexually active has been declining. For example, the Youth Risk Behavior Survey (YRBS) shows that the number of high school students who have ever had sexual intercourse fell from 54.1% in 1991 to 47.4% in 2011. The YRBS data also confirm that it is rare for kids to have sex for the first time before age 13 (6.2% in 2011, down from 10.2% in 1991).[4]

Thus, claims that today's kids engage in sex at radically younger ages are simply untrue; to the contrary, more teens are waiting longer to have their first sexual experiences. What's more, kids in the U.S. are behaving in very much the same way as their counterparts in other countries. In Canada, Australia, and Great Britain, the median age at first sex is between 16 and 17.[5]

Although today's teens first experience intercourse a year or so earlier than their grandparents did, recent trends show teens becoming sexually active later, not earlier. The widespread impression that today's teens are more likely to become sexually active at dramatically younger ages than ever before is simply mistaken.

Are Today's Teens More Promiscuous than in Previous Generations?

Sometimes it happens serially, that is, a teenager has sex with one partner, then another, then another, like an adult going through a series of divorces. But sometimes they have sex with several—or many—partners at once, either concurrently or . . . during group sex.

—Meg Meeker, *Epidemic*, 2002

Promiscuity is a loaded topic. Young people today do acquire more sexual partners than they did in their grandparents' day, but not necessarily because they are more promiscuous so much as because they stay single longer. In previous generations, people married much younger. So a girl coming of age around 1960 could expect to marry by 20, while a guy could expect to marry by 22. The prospect of early marriage, restricted access to birth control, and general societal disapproval of premarital sex helped keep the average number of sexual partners fairly low.[6] In 2011, the median age at first marriage in the U.S. reached an all-time high—26.5 for women and 28.7 for men.[7] With most young people having their first sexual experience in their late teens but not getting married for about a decade, it is almost inevitable that today's young people will have more sexual partners. But these partners are not necessarily acquired in one's teen years.

There are two basic ways that researchers try and track this question. The first is to ask teens how many different sexual partners they had in the previous 12 months. For instance, the NSFG for the years 2006–10 found that when females aged 15–19 were asked about their number of male partners in the previous year, 61.0% said they had not had sex (57.4% said they had never had sex, while 3.6% said they were sexually experienced but had not had a sexual partner during the past 12 months). Another 24.8% said they had had only one partner. That is, nearly 86% said they either had not had intercourse or had been monogamous during that period. The researchers noted, "The distribution of opposite-sex lifetime partners in 2006–2010 is comparable to those found in the 1988, 1995, and 2002 NSFGs."[8] In other words, over the past 20 years, the number of teens' sexual partners has not risen. A second measure—the proportion of teens who have had four or more sexual partners of the opposite sex—is used to track the riskiest behavior. Among high school students surveyed in 2011, 15.3% reported that they had had four or more sexual partners in their lifetime; this was down from 18.7% in 1991.[9]

Claims that today's teens have sex with a different partner every weekend do not find support in the available data. The number of partners teens have has remained relatively stable and has even declined a bit.

Is There an Oral-Sex Epidemic among Teens?

Many [young people] engage in [oral sex] rather cavalierly with friends, or even people they barely know. Sharing each other's genitals has become like sharing a cigarette, drink or joint in some circles.

—Dr. Ruth, as quoted in the *Globe and Mail*, 2008

The rainbow-party legend tapped into a broader concern that oral sex has become increasingly common and casual among teens.[10] It seems that everybody knows that today's kids view oral sex as a substitute for vaginal sex that allows them to maintain their "technical virginity," and they are having oral sex with large numbers of partners.

Once again, the data do not support what everybody knows. There is some evidence that young people are less likely to define oral sex as "sex." Two surveys of university students that posed the question found that the percentage classifying oral sex as sex fell from about 40% in 1991 to 20% in 2007.[11] On the other hand, there is little evidence that oral sex is rampant among the young or that lots of teens are participating in oral sex instead of intercourse. The NFSG data for 2007–10 show that among females ages 15–17, just over a quarter (27.4%) report having given oral sex—less than the 31.4% who say they have had vaginal intercourse.[12] There is some evidence that teens experience oral sex first; just over half of women say they had oral sex before their initial experience with intercourse. However, most teens who have had oral sex are the same people who have had sexual intercourse; among females 15–17, only about 7% report that they have had oral sex but not vaginal intercourse.[13] Thus, experience with oral sex resembles experience with sexual intercourse: it involves only a minority of younger teens and increases with age. The data do not support the notion that there is some sort of contemporary oral-sex epidemic among the young.

Are Today's Teens Having Casual or Anonymous Sex?

[The definition of *friends with benefits*] has expanded to mean having a sexual relationship with someone a teen may be tangentially friends with —it's more like friends of friends with benefits.
—Sabrina Weill, *The Real Truth about Teens and Sex*, 2005

Everybody also knows that young people casually choose to have indiscriminate sex, that whoever snaps off their jelly bracelet or shows up at the rainbow party can be their next sexual partner. In reality, most teens who are sexually active are in monogamous relationships—they are boyfriends and girlfriends. Of course, these relationships do not last forever, and after a relationship ends, a teen may find someone new and then engage in sexual behavior within that intimate relationship.[14] One study of teenagers reported that the majority of teens, 70% of females and 56% of males, indicated that their first sexual intercourse was with someone with whom they were "going steady."[15] And it's not just the first time; when males were asked to recall their nonmarital sexual relationships, they said that, on average, more than 70% were romantic; for females, the figure was more than 80%.[16] Teen sex occurs, on the whole, within the context of romantic relationships.

This is not to say that things haven't changed. It's true that young people today enter into relationships—that is, they find sexual and romantic partners—in different ways than previous generations did. The hookup has replaced the traditional date among both high school and college students, but there are many misperceptions about what a hookup involves. When young people today engage in a hookup encounter, it does not necessarily mean that they have sexual intercourse. Many hookups involve "just kissing" or "making out," and it is common for young people, particularly young women, to hope that a hookup will evolve into an ongoing relationship.[17]

Data from studies in other countries point to the same conclusion. For example, in a major Canadian study of over 10,000 students, those who had experienced sexual intercourse were asked their motivation for doing so, and the most common response was, "out of love for the person." In the United Kingdom, the majority of young people have their first sexual experience with someone they regard as a boyfriend or girlfriend. In Australia, less than 10% of those between the ages of 16 and 20 have had sex with more than two people whom they did not consider themselves to be "seriously dating." So neither the research on the U.S. hookup scene nor the data in other Western countries supports the idea that *typical* teen sex involves engaging in anonymous or random sexual encounters.[18]

Thus, although many teens are sexually active, both in the U.S. and abroad, the hype about sex and today's kids has been grossly misleading. The age that teens begin having sex has not gotten dramatically younger in recent decades, most teens are not having sex with a large number of partners, and they are not engaging in frequent, anonymous sexual intercourse or oral-sex orgies. Furthermore, when it comes to sexual behavior, teens in the U.S. are not dissimilar to teens in other English-speaking countries.

Why All the Fuss?

If the empirical data on youth and sex do not match what everybody thinks they know, we need to ask why contemporary legends and other exaggerated messages about kids gone wild persist. Here, it will help to consider how various sectors of society benefit from either making these claims or allowing them to continue unchecked.

Kids/Teens

Anyone familiar with kids and teens knows that they spend a lot of time discussing the sexual or romantic behavior of their classmates and friends. At younger ages, a large part of socializing revolves around teasing each other about who "like-likes" whom, who is a couple, and who is going to get married someday. As kids get older and begin to engage in minor forms of sexual activity, such as kissing or making out, the gossip turns to finding out how far a couple went sexually and whether a pair has become a "Facebook official" couple (i.e., whether each party has changed his or her relationship status on Facebook to indicate that he or she is in a relationship).[19]

Given teens' preoccupation with each other, it is easy to see how a rumor about a sex-bracelet or rainbow-party scandal can quickly spread through a school. What could be more exciting than talking about how a friend of a friend knows someone who knows someone who had a rainbow party last night? It is also easy to spread a story that a classmate's red jelly bracelet means that she gives lap dances. In the age of the Internet, these stories don't just travel via traditional word of mouth at a school or within a friendship circle. Instead, they can go viral on the Internet—through Facebook comments, for example. And the more the rumor gets retold, the harder it is to kill. In other words, as a legend becomes familiar, it gains traction.

In addition to kids enjoying gossiping both in person and online about sex bracelets, rainbow parties, and sexting, there is perhaps another purpose that these legends and other exaggerated stories about teens and sex serve. That is, they help young people rationalize their own behavior. At this age, young people are still forming their sense of who they are and who they want to be. They are looking to their classmates to see what kind of behavior is "normal," and they are listening to their friends and classmates to ascertain which behaviors are not accepted by their peers, for example, who is a "good girl" and who is a "bad girl." This is why some teens accept the stories of other kids' wild parties or sex games as true, although they insist that they, themselves, never engage in the rumored behavior. It is always *other* students who play the sex-bracelet game and really perform the sex acts or *other* students who are the ones attending rainbow parties. The legend proliferates because it allows kids and teens to conclude that whatever they are doing sexually is not as bad as what *other* kids are doing.

This point is illustrated by a letter that appeared in a Baton Rouge newspaper. Writing to a columnist who had mentioned sex bracelets, a 17-year-old male high school student responded that he had talked to other kids at conferences and youth organizations and had discovered who is "really" doing the sex-bracelet game and who is not: "On the Eastern seaboard, the connotation of these bracelets with sexual acts is very heavy, and the teens often follow through. In Louisiana, these rumors are baseless. No one I've ever spoken with from here has ever heard of or witnessed this 'ritual' being followed. The bracelets are just a simple fashion statement."[20]

In other words, stories about kids exploring the boundaries of sexuality not only offer entertaining subjects for conversation; they also allow teens opportunities to affirm their own identities—whether those are edgy or more conventional.

Parents

Because many parents are concerned about a wide variety of people, places, and things that could harm their children, they serve as perfect targets for much of the media hype surrounding teens and sex, especially in the context of the new intensive parenting.[21] Many media stories on rainbow parties and sex bracelets were targeted directly to parents. Consider these examples, taken from both TV news coverage and newspaper articles and from the United States, England, Canada, and Australia:

> Well, parents beware. Your teenage daughter's favorite accessory may be a kind of sexual code.[22]

> THOUSANDS OF YOUNG CHILDREN ARE BUYING THESE COLOURED WRISTBANDS EVERY WEEK. BUT PARENTS HAVE NO IDEA OF THEIR TRUE DISTURBING MEANING.[23]

> They're called "shag bands" and they are . . . a parent's worst nightmare.[24]

> If drinking, driving, and college admissions aren't enough for the parents of teenagers to worry about, there's a new specter on the horizon: "rainbow parties."[25]

> Dads across North America are going ballistic when they discover that their darling daughters have joined the Rainbow Club.[26]

The sex-bracelet and rainbow-party stories gave parents a way to talk about their fears about kids and sex, especially fears about their daughters. They allowed parents to believe that the kids they hear about through these stories might be a corrupting influence on their innocent, naive children. Just as teens who use the distorted image of youth culture as a way to draw lines between themselves (the good kids) and others (the bad kids), parents have a tendency to do the same. There are countless media stories in which a parent confirms the existence of either the sex-bracelet game or rainbow parties while maintaining that it is not *their* kids who participate. For example, a father from Pennsylvania who learned about sex bracelets from his daughter describes them as a "left-coast trend": "[My daughter] told me from the height of her 12-year old worldliness, kids in California were apparently using them in a game —boys would snap theirs, girls would snap theirs and whichever pair had them break first would have sex. Makes spin the bottle seem quaint, doesn't it?"[27] Many parents are not just aware of but believe stories about teenage sexuality as a societal phenomenon, yet they manage to argue that their own children are not part of this pattern: "Other teenagers may be sexual, even hypersexual, engaging in risky and promiscuous sexual behavior, but their own children, regardless of age or actual behavior, are 'not that kind of kid.' "[28] Tales of troubling teen behavior, then, can reassure parents about their own children's goodness or even their own daughters' relative purity.

School Officials

While it is understandable that kids and their parents might buy into the hype about teen sex, it is less obvious why school officials seem to jump on the bandwagon. It would seem to serve their interests to portray their schools in the most positive light by projecting an image of students who are well behaved and engrossed in their academic pursuits. So why do school officials—at least those quoted in media reports—always seem to say that parents should be very concerned about the supposedly wild behavior of their kids?

Perhaps school officials do not want either to appear out of the loop regarding what is "really" going on in their schools or to seem unresponsive to the rumored exploits of their students. Additionally, since parents would likely be outraged if administrators failed to inform them of a "dangerous sex game" that was happening at their school, officials are under pressure to alert parents when they hear these tales. Thus, a school board member who appeared on *Dr. Phil* explained, "Bracelets are stimulating conversation, which has proven to be disruptive. We've had cases in our schools where it has been disruptive, and that's why one of my teams of administrators at one of our schools did ban the bracelets."[29]

In addition to wanting to appear "on top of things," administrators might also feel compelled to educate students when a controversial issue about kids and sex begins to receive a lot of attention. If they too believe the hype, they probably figure they ought to address the issue with students and reassure anxious parents. In doing so, however, they end up lending credence to the claims, thereby perpetuating the story.

Media

Journalists and other members of the media played a key role in spreading the rainbow-party and sex-bracelet stories. Throughout this book, we have shown how both print and electronic media informed the public about these legends by presenting exaggerated depictions of youth and sex and arguing that parents and society at large should be worried about today's kids. Why would journalists do this? Obviously, sex sells: such stories are believed to sell papers and win high television ratings. But in addition to the media's attempts to gain readers and attract viewers with sensationalistic headlines and stories about kids gone wild, these stories tapped into parents' and society's fears. Not only does sex sell, but so does fearmongering.

To be sure, media outlets varied in their enthusiasm for sensational coverage. The major television-network news programs—which claim high journalistic standards—never covered sex bracelets and only mentioned rainbow parties in a single story about the controversy surrounding the novel *Rainbow Party*. Most television coverage occurred in what is sometimes called infotainment—on the networks' morning programs, on talk shows, and on the programs hosted by cable news pundits. This coverage tended to be credulous, treating these tales as growing trends among youth. In contrast, print journalists were more likely to present skeptical views and acknowledge that at least some people considered the stories about sex bracelets and rainbow parties to be urban legends. And as we demonstrated in chapter 4, the Internet allowed both believers and skeptics to debate both subjects. The skewed nature of the media coverage of sex bracelets and rainbow parties becomes more apparent when it is contrasted with the treatment of sexting. Sexting received far more—and for more nuanced—coverage than either of the other two stories did. However, even the sexting stories were often sensationalistic, presenting the most extreme cases along with claims that "everyone was doing it." Particularly in the case of television coverage, it seems ratings were prioritized over accuracy or evidence.

Advocates

It is also important to note that media reports often used experts or other advocates as sources to affirm that kids really were going wild. In particular, social and religious conservatives used stories about sex bracelets and rainbow parties to support their positions. Meg Meeker, whose book *Epidemic: How Teen Sex Is Killing Our Kids* made the first mention of rainbow parties, is a physician but also a conservative commentator, and her book was published by a conservative press.[30] The stories were also relayed in books aimed at young readers from religious publishers.[31] Warnings about rainbow parties and sex bracelets were consistent with conservatives' calls for a less sexualized popular culture, abstinence-based sex education, and other methods for protecting the vulnerable young. Liberal advocates tended to frame their comments in terms of feminist critiques of a sexist culture that disadvantaged girls.

Experts—particularly legislators, criminal justice authorities, and legal scholars—were more likely to weigh in on sexting because people could point to actual cases that had implications for the First Amendment, enforcement of child pornography and sex offender laws, and so on. Vendors of software and technology claimed that their products might help parents manage their children's sexting. All these figures proved willing to add their voices to the media's reports about new trends in teen sex.

Why We Like to Talk about Kids Gone Wild

In sum, lots of folks—not just the media and advocates but also teens, parents, and educators—have reasons to damp down their skepticism and repeat reports of out-of-control youth involved in sex bracelets, rainbow parties, and sexting. Moreover, these claims tapped into a broader cultural concern about the sexualization of young people—the idea that kids are becoming too sexy too soon.

That is, there are claims that kids are thinking about sex, talking about sex, and engaging in sex at younger and younger ages. Commentators agreed on this overarching problem of the sexualization of youth; however, they framed this argument in two contrasting ways that reflected the larger culture wars. For the most part, liberals focused attention on young girls as the victims of a sexualized culture, while conservatives saw the problem as reflecting the deterioration of family values, especially declining morality in young girls.

Victimization of Girls

When some commentators discussed sex bracelets, rainbow parties, or sexting, they shifted the focus from all kids to *girls*. Liberals/feminists used these stories as evidence of girls being harassed, degraded, and abused: girls having their jelly bracelets snapped off and then being goaded into engaging in various sexual acts; girls attending rainbow parties in order to service and please their male classmates at the expense of their own well-being; and girls being encouraged to sext nude photos of themselves to their male classmates only to have those photos forwarded to many others so that the female sender winds up humiliated, bullied, or even in trouble with the law.

The *sexualization* of childhood has drawn the attention of psychologists and other academics. This term is broad and encompasses everything from Bratz dolls to sexual abuse:

> Societal messages that contribute to the sexualization of girls come not only from media and merchandise but also through girls' interpersonal relationships. . . . Parents may contribute to sexualization in a number of ways. For example, parents may convey the message that maintaining an attractive physical appearance is the most important goal for girls. . . . If girls purchase (or ask their parents to purchase) products and clothes designed to make them look physically appealing and sexy, and if they style their identities after the sexy celebrities who populate their cultural landscape, they are, in effect, sexualizing themselves. Girls also sexualize themselves when they think of themselves in objectified terms. Psychological researchers have identified *self-objectification* as a key process whereby girls learn to think of and treat their own bodies as objects of others' desires.[32]

The concern about sexualization provided a context for interpreting reports of sex bracelets, rainbow parties, and sexting. Claims that sex play was a form of pressure on girls came from all sorts of authorities and from all English-speaking countries. In Canada, a psychiatrist who heads McGill University's Mental Health Services argued that rainbow parties "are a form of abuse and degradation of young women. What do they get out of it? . . . Mostly low self-esteem."[33] In Australia, a "cyber safety expert"—a former police officer working in schools—called shag bands "appalling": "I think it's disgusting and it is just another example of the overt sexualisation of young people. . . . People may say it's just like spin the bottle but it's not. This game puts a huge amount of pressure on young girls to be sexually active."[34] Similar claims were made by feminists when discussing sexting. On NPR's program *Tell Me More*, panelists were invited to comment on an extreme sexting case that made the news (a teen girl had been taped performing oral sex, and that video was posted on Facebook and other public sites). One panelist—Malika Saada Saar, an activist—framed the issue this way: "And I think it plays into a larger culture that says it is okay to objectify very young girls as sexual objects. It is okay to say that very young girls are sexually available. I mean we have push-up bras for 10-year-olds and thongs for 7-year-olds. There is a gathering culture that without question hypersexualizes very young girls."[35]

Deterioration of Family Values

While critiques of sexualization often came from liberal feminists, some conservative commentators adopted very similar language. From the conservative point of view, teens—and particularly girls—have abandoned traditional moral standards. Conservatives see many signs that family values are not as strong as they used to be; divorce rates, out-of-wedlock births, and gay marriage are all interpreted as evidence that the family is in trouble. From this perspective, reports of sex bracelets, rainbow parties, and sexting are simply further proof that society is, indeed, in jeopardy.

Conservative commentators often underscore that things are getting worse; they nostalgically recall a different world during their own youth:

I'm both happy and resentful to report that so-called rainbow parties—reportedly a real-life trend—are a new one on me: Happy that I've lived multiple decades without an inkling, resentful that I'm now and forever stuck with the knowledge. Who needs it?[36]

I'm 33 but I can say "That would have been impossible when I was a kid." Every day, a new low point is reached. Lipsticks for group oral sex, bracelets to indicate what sex acts you're willing to perform . . . organized, marketed, publicized madness.[37]

Similarly, when conservatives analyzed sexting, they often characterized the phenomenon as a sign that teen behavior is getting worse: "Sexting is a result of mainstream acceptance of sexuality and a lack of forced morality by parents. There's a degree of sexual expression that's completely atypical of years past. It's a direct consequence of having no uniform set of commonly shared moral values. Things are blurred for kids now. They experiment with sexuality with the computer and cell phone."[38]

Like feminists, conservative commentators blamed facets of popular culture, including toys, fashion, music, and the Internet, for promoting sexualized visions of childhood. In this view, the larger culture encourages children to think about sex, so it is no wonder that they discover disturbing new forms of sexual play.

Conclusion

Obviously, there is nothing new, either in worrying about the safety and well-being of the young or in having concerns about young people misbehaving. The rise of modern societies has given young people more individual freedom, including the chance to choose among an ever-wider array of tastes, products, and identities. Generations of adults have found it difficult to interpret the meaning of youth culture, with its new vocabulary and new enthusiasms, new music and new dances, new dress and grooming styles, and so on, even as children choose new cultural forms as a way to establish themselves as different from their parents. When those children age, they will recall those symbols of their youth with nostalgia and marvel that their parents bothered worrying so much about so little. But at the same time, those former children, when faced with the new confusing signals being sent by their own kids, may find it difficult not to worry.

Of course, sex is often near the center of these concerns about changes in youth culture. Commentators talk about a sexual revolution, even as sociologists speak of "shifting sexual scripts." Who knows what today's kids may be up to, what sorts of new, threatening, dangerous sexual practices may be spreading among the young? Generations of adults have worried about petting parties, going steady, and—in our new millennium—about sex bracelets, rainbow parties, and sexting.

Certainly parents have a right to be concerned about their own children—that their daughters may get pregnant or that their sons will cause a pregnancy, that they will catch a sexually transmitted disease, or that their activities may lead to physical, emotional, or spiritual harms— just as it is appropriate for public health officials to be concerned about risky sex among teens. But contemporary legends and exaggerated fears don't help. Rather, these stories give a distorted view of youth and make it more difficult for parents or others who work with young people.

Perhaps one of the most misleading things about these exaggerated claims is that they promote the idea that dangerous sexual practices are widespread, that they occur throughout society, so that people are left with the impression that every kid is *equally* likely to engage in worrisome sexual behavior or to suffer one of the consequences associated with it. As Meg Meeker puts it,

> We're not talking about troubled teens: We're talking about *all* teens— yours and mine. The teens who belong to the church youth group, work at the local gas station, or hand you ice cream across the counter. They have personalities and faces. Look at their faces and see who you think might be infected [with an STD]. If you look at more than five, chances are you'll see at least one infected with a horrible disease. Black, white, Asian, Hispanic. Rich kids or poor. Straight-A students or dropouts. It doesn't matter. Sexually transmitted viruses, bacteria and parasites don't discriminate. They attack all sexually active teens.[39]

Such claims ignore much of what we know about the patterns of sexual behavior among the young. The data demonstrate that not every kid is equally likely to have sex at a young age, have multiple partners, get pregnant, or contract a sexually transmitted disease. In the U.S. and other developed countries, adolescents from lower-income families tend to have sex somewhat earlier than do their counterparts from middle- or high-income families.[40] Likewise, African American adolescents (who are overrepresented among the poor) are more likely to have intercourse at younger ages than are adolescents from Hispanic or white backgrounds. For example, data from the 2011 YRBS show the disparate breakdown by race of high school students reporting having had intercourse: blacks, 60%; Hispanics, 48.6%; and whites, 44.3%. Blacks and Hispanics also are more likely than their white counterparts are to have had sex prior to age 13 (blacks, 13.9%; Hispanics, 7.1%; whites, 3.9%) and to have had four or more partners (blacks, 24.8%; Hispanics, 14.8%; whites, 13.1%).[41]

Given that members of ethnic minorities are more likely than whites to engage in high-risk sexual behavior, it is not surprising that they also are far more likely to get a sexually transmitted disease. For example, according to the Centers for Disease Control, 70% of youths ages 13–19 who were diagnosed with HIV/AIDS in 2006 were black, compared to 14% Hispanic and 14% white. A similar pattern holds true among other sexually transmitted diseases. In fact, according to the CDC, "Racial minorities . . . face severe disparities across all three reportable STDs. . . . African-Americans, especially young African-American women, are the most heavily affected. Young African-American women face significantly higher rates of chlamydia and gonorrhea than any other group, while the highest rates of syphilis are among African-American men."[42]

A similar pattern is found in national data on teen pregnancy. Both African American and Hispanic teens are significantly more likely than their white counterparts to give birth during their teen years, a statistic that again reflects minorities being overrepresented among the poor. However, like much of the trend data we examined earlier in the chapter, which showed that contemporary teens are less sexually active than teens were 20 years ago, the teen birthrate in 2009 was 37% lower than it was in 1991.[43]

The point in highlighting racial/ethnic differences in sexual behavior is *not* that minorities are the kids who are "really" going wild sexually. Rather, the sex-bracelet and rainbow-party legends, and the media coverage of teen sex in general, have been used to fuel the fears of white, middle-class parents that their kids are engaging in unprecedented sexual promiscuity. In doing so, the media ignores real class differences in sexual behavior, which are connected to poverty, educational opportunities, and other complex factors that the news media, particularly television, often want to avoid in favor of more sensationalistic stories.

In addition to class and ethnicity affecting sexual activity among youth, so does the type of family in which adolescents are raised. For example, studies indicate that teens in the U.S. are significantly less likely to be sexually experienced if

- their mother had her first birth at age 20 or over;
- their mother was a college graduate; and
- they lived with both parents.

According to the National Survey on Family Growth, 35% of female teens who lived with both parents were sexually experienced, compared with 54% among those who lived in any other parental arrangement.[44] Further, research shows that parents' making their feelings about teen sex known to their kids also makes a difference.[45] Similarly, teens who are very religious are less sexually active,[46] while those who drink alcohol regularly are more sexually active.[47]

The point is that youths' sexual behavior is patterned, that risks are not evenly—or randomly—distributed. Moreover, many of the patterns reflect factors, such as the socioeconomic status of teens' parents, outside their control. This stands in stark contrast to claims that the principal forces driving teens' sexual behavior emanate from pop culture's sexual messages. To be sure, teens make choices. But those choices are shaped both by individuals' location within the larger social structure—by class and ethnicity—and, importantly, by their families. Teens make choices, but their choices are also structured by parental influence regarding religiosity and drinking. And parents influence their kids' sexual choices by communicating that they care about the issue.

In the final analysis, it is not only important for parents to educate themselves about what young people are (and are not) doing. It is also important for adults in general—teachers, administrators, counselors, health professionals, and others who care about the well-being of youth —to understand how to sort through the stories and media reports they hear about "these kids today." We hope this book has not only shed light on the rumored sexual exploits of teens but also suggested ways of thinking about such claims. For there are sure to be more of these stories. It is not enough to debunk particular tales as exaggerations, for new stories about kids gone wild persist. A story that is snuffed out in one location can pop up somewhere else; or a new story, equally as dubious, can come along to take its place. So we need to become critical consumers of claims about what the younger generation is doing. If not, we will continue to make the mistake of falling for the next legend or hyped story. As blogger Maureen Henderson put it, "Clutching our pearls and imploring others to please think of the children never goes out of style."[48] The younger generation deserves better than how we talk about them. It's the adults that need to wise up.

NOTES

NOTES TO THE PREFACE

1. According to Sinikka Elliott (2012), parents are inclined to believe that other kids are hypersexual and pose a danger to their own child but are resistant to the idea that their own kid is a sexual being. As a result, parents are ripe for news stories that warn them about the dangers other kids pose if they don't watch out.
2. *The Today Show*, NBC, November 14, 2008.
3. Schudson (2011: 30).
4. Kliff (2013).

NOTES TO CHAPTER 1

1. Best (1990); Jenkins (1998); Leon (2011).
2. *Shag* has been slang for sexual intercourse since the eighteenth century, although it is more commonly used in Britain than in the United States (Partridge 1970: 748).
3. The expression *jelly bracelet* may allude both to the gel plastic and also to sex. *Jelly* has been part of sexual slang at least since the seventeenth century (Partridge 1970: 435). A contemporary example is the lyric "I don't think you ready for this jelly" in Destiny's Child's "Bootylicious."
4. The bracelets date back to at least the 1980s; one informant recalled that female students in her high school supposedly wore black gel bracelets to indicate how many times they had had sex. This is itself a variant of other stories about teens wearing items of particular colors to indicate they are sexually active; for example, *The Yellow Teddybears* (a 1963 film) was based on news reports that females in an English school wore yellow golliwogs to indicate that they were no longer virgins. Robert MacGregor (2012) explores the tale—spread by both children and adults—that green M&Ms are an aphrodisiac. The bracelets' association of particular colors with different sexual acts also resembles the handkerchief code used by male homosexuals (Gay City USA 2011; Newall 1986).

5. Liebau (2007: 18). For examples of stories featuring elementary-school-age children, see Garvey and Campanile (2004); Pearce (2009).

6. "Is Your Child Leading a Double Life?, " *The Oprah Winfrey Show*, syndicated, October 1, 2003.

7. Ruditis (2005).

8. Wolfe (2000: 7).

9. Flanagan (2006: 167); Liebau (2007: 22–23); see also Young (2006). These reports were disturbing, in part, because they depicted groups of adolescents participating in organized occasions for *consensual* oral sex. Train parties, described as involving several boys and girls, should not be confused with the expression *pulling a train*, which according to the *Oxford English Dictionary* dates back at least to the 1930s and refers to several males having sexual intercourse with one female. Most analysts—and the women involved—view these occasions as coercive, although Jody Miller (2008) notes that young African American males who *run trains* (multiple males having sex with a female) consider this activity consensual.

10. Reitz (2008).

11. Sutton-Smith (1959: 208, 209); see also Epstein (1999); Roud (2010); Thorne (1993); Tucker (2008).

12. NFBSK (2009).

13. Whiting (1945).

14. Maurer (1976).

15. Bogle (2008).

16. *New York Times* (1922: 1). On the concern with petting, see Fass (1977).

17. Bailey (2004: 25). See also Barclay (1960); Whitbread (1957).

18. On reactions to the effects of social changes on sexual behavior, see Bailey (1988); D'Emilio and Freedman (1988). On concerns about the sexual dangers of music, see Martin and Segrave (1988).

19. On the emergence of the pragmatic position, see D'Emilio and Freedman (1988). For a contemporary, critical version, see Males (2010).

20. Philip Jenkins (2006) argues that public attitudes toward many social issues became more conservative during the late 1970s. On the longer history on concerns about protecting children, see Beisel (1997); Jenkins (1998); Kincaid (1998): Malón (2011).

21. Durham (2008); Levin and Kilbourne (2008); Liebau (2007); Olfman (2009).

22. This alliance is hardly unprecedented. Conservatives have made common cause with some feminists over other sexual issues, including pornography (D. Downs 1989), child sexual abuse (Jenkins 1998), and human trafficking (Bernstein 2010).

23. For examples, see Ferguson (2000); Fields (2005); J. Irvine (2002, 2006); Luker (2006).

24. Nelson (2010). For a parallel British analysis, see Furedi (2001).

25. J. Irvine (2002); Luker (2006).

26. Martin and Segrave (1988). Research on adolescents' exposure to and use of

sexual messages in mass media suggests that youth have a far less passive and more complicated relationship to media (Brown, Steele, and Walsh-Childers 2002).

27. BBC News (2009). This was a rumor; there was no evidence that the bracelets had sexually explicit packaging.

28. Berry (2009).

29. Beresin (2010); Opie and Opie (1959); Roud (2010); Sutton-Smith (1972); Tucker (2008).

30. Critiques of play include Carlsson-Page and Levin (1990); Epstein (1999); Murnen and Smolak (2000); Renold (2002); and Thorne (1993). On the campaign against competitive games, see Grineski (1996); Williams (1994).

31. Schulte (2008); Urbina (2009).

32. There is a large literature on legend and rumor, including Brunvand (2001); Ellis (2001); Fine, Campion-Vincent, and Heath (2005); and Fine and Ellis (2010). Folklorists draw a clear distinction between legends and myths; myths are origin stories about gods and goddesses. However convenient journalists may find the shorter word when composing headlines, there are no urban myths.

33. Best (2013) offers an overview of how social problems are constructed.

34. What has become a large literature on moral panics was launched by Stanley Cohen ([1972] 2002). Recent works include Goode and Ben-Yehuda (2009); Hier (2011), Krinsky (2013). On sex panics, see Elliott (2010); Herdt (2009); J. Irvine (2006); Lancaster (2011).

NOTES TO CHAPTER 2

1. Brunvand (1981).

2. Folklorists restrict the term *myth* to refer to sacred stories about the remote past; their principal characters are usually gods or animals (think of Greek mythology). According to Brunvand, "There is little, if any, need for the term 'myth' in urban-legend studies" (2001: 279). *Big Urban Myth Show* was on MTV during 2002–4; *Urban Legends* began on the Biography Channel in 2007 and was resurrected on Syfy in 2011; *Mythbusters* began on the Discovery Channel in 2003.

3. For example, Alan Dundes and Carl Pagter (1975) collected several compilations of photocopied office folklore. Trevor Blank (2009) and Bill Ellis (2003) illustrate folklorists' approaches to online lore.

4. Brunvand (2001: 466–67).

5. On racial transformations in legends, see Langlois (1983); and Fine and Turner (2001). On tales about dangerous imports, see Fine and Ellis (2010).

6. Allport and Postman (1947).

7. Heath, Bell, and Sternberg (2001).

8. "The common conception of the origin of rumor maintains it is impossible to establish the creator (as it is for most items of folklore)" (Rosnow and Fine 1976: 24). In contrast, topical joke cycles—jokes that spring up following some

newsworthy event—make it possible to identify a date before which there could have been no jokes; for example, jokes about the explosion of the space shuttle *Challenger* could not have spread before January 28, 1986. There have been efforts to document the spread of such jokes (Ellis 1991, 2003; Kurti 1988; Lowney and Best 1996).

9. For introductions to general methodological issues involved in doing Internet research, see Hine (2000, 2005).

10. We used four search terms to locate comments about sex bracelets: "gel brace-let," "jelly bracelet," "sex bracelet," and "shag bands"; in contrast, we judged that the search terms "rainbow party" and "rainbow parties" would be sufficient. We searched several databases: (1) the full-text databases Lexis-Nexis Academic and NewsBank Newspapers, which allowed us to identify newspaper articles and broadcast transcripts from major media outlets; (2) OneFile (a general database for periodicals), a search that turned up few sources not independently identi-fied through the Lexis-Nexis search; (3) Google Scholar, which identified sev-eral books, articles, and pamphlets that mentioned—usually only briefly—sex bracelets and rainbow parties, as well as a single scholarly article on the former topic (Weaver 2005); and (4) scholarly databases such as America: History and Life, Criminal Justice Abstracts, ERIC, MEDLINE, PsycInfo, and Sociological Abstracts, searches that failed to locate any additional sources.

We also used the Google search engine to search the web, and we surveyed dozens of Facebook pages dedicated to shag bands. Unlike other sources of Inter-net comments in our sample, Facebook was only launched after the shag-band and rainbow-party stories began to spread, in early 2004 (when it was largely limited to students at selected university campuses). It did not become gener-ally available to anyone with an email address until 2006. We identified several hundred pages featuring titles about "shag bands," "sex bracelets," and the like and included 100 in our sample; those we coded tended to have the largest number of people reporting they "liked" the page. There were many fewer Facebook pages devoted to rainbow parties, and none are included in our sample of comments. In all cases, we sought to identify the earliest date when pages began operating.

In addition, we identified still more sources from regional newspapers or local television broadcasts, and we further checked various websites dedicated to contemporary legends (although all of these proved to have been identified in our Google search). Legends and Rumors, a website that posts instances of recent press coverage, identified stories about sex bracelets (Chapman 2010), and Brian Chapman, who maintains the website, also kindly shared his personal files regarding press treatments of rainbow parties. Colleagues assisted us by conduct-ing foreign-language searches for coverage of sex bracelets in Brazil, Germany, Italy, Korea, and the Netherlands. Our searches located a variety of sources dealing with extraneous topics (e.g., for sex bracelets: electronic bracelets worn by convicted sex offenders, bracelets used in sexual bondage, shag bands as a type of southern musical group; for rainbow parties: various political movements that adopted rainbow-related names or symbols, rainbow-themed children's parties), and we eliminated these from our sample.

11. Private, post on Lexington Forum, June 2, 2010; Niamh, post on Facebook, September 1, 2008.

12. Meeker (2002: 22–23).

13. Howey (2003: 219).

14. This episode inspired a good deal of commentary; see Flanagan (2006); Gregory (2010); Young (2006).

15. Ruditis (2005). For an example of the reactions to the novel, see Malkin (2005).

16. Picoult (2006).

17. For example, see Wells (2004).

18. momlogic (2008).

19. Vega, "rainbow party," definition 3, *Urban Dictionary*, posted October 4, 2003, http://www.urbandictionary.com/define.php?term=rainbow+party (retrieved December 30, 2013); see also BRD, "Rainbow Parties." definition 7, *Urban Dictionary*, posted July 10, 2005, http://www.urbandictionary.com/define.php?term=rainbow+party (retrieved December 30, 2013).

20. Fine (1992); Whatley and Henken (2000).

21. Train parties were discussed in chapter 1. "Parties where oral sex predominates are sometimes called 'chicken parties,' because of the way all the girls' heads are bobbing up and down as they go down on their partner-of-the-moment" (Sax 2005: 119). According to the *Urban Dictionary*, stoneface is "a game in which a group of males, sitting around a table, get oral sex from one female under the table . . . the object of the game is to show no emotion." DoubleD, "stoneface," definition 2, *Urban Dictionary*, posted February 28, 2005, http://www.urbandictionary.com/define.php?term=stoneface (retrieved December 30, 2013); ellipsis in original.

   Tales of this sort are not new; one reader of this manuscript recalled, "There was a great rumor in my high school that a girl went 'skiing'—that is, she supposedly gave hand jobs to two boys and a blow job to the guy in the middle all at the same time mimicking the ski motion."

22. "Lipstick on Your Panties," *Huff*, Showtime, November 1, 2004; "Over the Rainbow," *The Hard Times of RJ Berger*, MTV, July 12, 2010.

23. For examples, see Gross and Foster (2005); Levy (2005); Sax (2005); and Weill (2005).

24. Junior, "shag band," definition 14, *Urban Dictionary*, posted September 22, 2003, http://www.urbandictionary.com/define.php?term=shag+band&page=2 (retrieved December 30, 2013). We quote posts verbatim, regardless of unorthodox spelling, spacing, abbreviations, and punctuation. Although care should be taken in deconstructing these texts, the use of "shag" and the spelling "colours" suggests that this post's author might have been British or Canadian.

25. Ressner (2003: 80).

26. *Education Coffeehouse Newsletter* (2003); NFBSK (2009).

27. Although we accessed many of these comments on websites operated by newspapers or television stations, we classified them as originating in traditional print/ broadcast media. When these stories inspired online discussion threads, the comments on those threads were not classified as involving traditional media.

28. Because shag bands were likely to be worn and talked about in school, it is not surprising that comments about the bracelets tended to occur during the school year. Throughout 2003–10, months between September and May averaged 25.7 comments—more than twice the 12.7 average for summer months.

29. For a vendor, see CafePress (2010). On the meanings of colors, see Fine et al. (1998).

30. Posts on Jonesboro Forum: Concerned, August 31, 2008; Whatever, August 31, 2008; Been There Done That, August 31, 2008; Used to have em, September 27, 2008; Star, October 3, 2008; Amy, November 24, 2008; who cares, February 3, 2009; juggalo 4 life 69420, February 10, 2009; katie, April 28, 2009; and crystal waters, June 9, 2009). However analytically tempting it might be to assume that black had racial connotations, the comment by "Used to have em" was the only comment in our sample that made this connection.

31. Of the 2,028 comments in our sample, 179 featured keys for the meanings of at least four colors. Some comments contained two or more keys. Our sample of keys contained mentions of 48 different colors. Keys were defined as belonging to the same variant so long as they shared meanings for all but one color. For instance, if Key A had meanings for only four colors, and Key B listed all of those meanings but also assigned a meaning for a fifth color, they were classified as belonging to the same variant. Similarly, if Key C listed the four same colors as Key A but gave a different meaning for one of those colors, the two keys were classified as belonging to the same variant. In practice, most keys assigned meanings for more than four colors (the median number of colors given meanings was 12), so that sharing all but one assigned meaning offered a fairly rigorous standard for identifying similarities.

32. Different keys used a variety of terms to denote this meaning, including "sex," "intercourse," "sexual intercourse," "full on sex," "regular sex," "missionary sex," "regular 'missionary' sex," "shag," "all the way," and "the full monty." A far older and widely used—albeit more vulgar—word was strikingly absent from *any* of the keys (Sheidlower 2009).

33. Sex-bracelets.com (2009). Although the page at Sex-bracelets.com accessed in 2010 features a 2009 copyright, a search via web.archive.org located a version (with the same color key) dated November 18, 2003. A number of 2003 newspaper articles attributed their meanings to the website.

34. Amyth.com (2003).

35. Six of the variants appeared only in a single year, but another six were found in keys at least five years apart, which meant that they emerged during the initial

2003–4 wave and endured to reappear in the later 2009–10 wave. Because many of the keys were posted on websites that made it impossible to be confident about their country of origin, evidence for the geographic diffusion of the variants is limited. However, of the six variants that endured for at least five years, three had clearly spread from the U.S. to other countries, and a fourth was only spotted in England in 2009, although it seems to have originated in North America in 2005. Five variants appeared in at least two countries; another five had confirmed locations only in a non-U.S. country, with all the keys with confirmed locations appearing during the second wave in 2009–10.

If we assume that a variant remained in circulation between its first appearance and its last, our evidence demonstrates that there were at least 3 variants in circulation in 2003, 6 between 2004 and 2006, 8 in 2007, 9 in 2008, 13 in 2009, and 9 in 2010. In general, the number of variants in circulation increased. However, some variants seemed to fall out of favor: in 2010, we did not locate keys containing 9— fully half—of the 18 variants. In general, variants did not become more elaborate over time; the mean number of colors assigned meanings in the three 2003 variants was 12.0, compared to 12.3 in the variants in circulation in 2010.

This sort of variation is not uncommon in contemporary legends. Bill Ellis (1994) examined 76 versions of the horror legend "The Hook" and found that only 57% featured what he classified as "typical narratives."

36. A. Downs (1972).
37. We collected these data in late 2013, so the table's coverage stops with 2012, the last full year. But it was clear that media attention of sexting would continue, at least into 2013 and possibly beyond, whereas coverage of rainbow parties and sex bracelets seems to have halted.
38. Hill (2010); M. Sherman (2011).

NOTES TO CHAPTER 3

1. On the nature of formulas, see Cawelti (1976). On the appeal of formulas for audiences, see Radway (1984).
2. Analyses of formulas and conventions that shape TV coverage include Gitlin (1983); Letukas (2012); and Lowney (1999).
3. *Scarborough Country*, MSNBC, November 13, 2003.
4. *The Today Show*, NBC, November 14, 2003.
5. *The Big Story with John Gibson*, Fox News, May 24, 2004.
6. *Scarborough Country*, MSNBC, May 25, 2004.
7. *Good Morning America*, ABC, May 26, 2004.
8. *American Morning*, CNN, July 5, 2005.
9. *The Situation with Tucker Carlson*, MSNBC, January 17, 2006.
10. M. Irvine (2003).
11. Lewin (2005: G1); see also Stepp (2004).
12. *Scarborough Country*, November 13, 2003.

13. *Scarborough Country*, May 25, 2004.
14. "Teen Sex: The Shocking Truth," *The Montel Williams Show*, syndicated, January 27, 2005.
15. "Is Your Child Leading a Double Life?," *The Oprah Winfrey Show*, syndicated, October 1, 2003.
16. "The Truth about Sex," *The Doctors*, syndicated, May 27, 2010.
17. *The Today Show*, November 14, 2003.
18. *Scarborough Country*, May 25, 2004.
19. *Good Morning America*, May 26, 2004; emphasis added.
20. *The Today Show*, November 14, 2003.
21. *The Big Story with John Gibson*, May 24, 2004.
22. *Scarborough Country*, May 25, 2004.
23. *The Today Show*, November 14, 2003.
24. "Girls Misbehaving," *Dr. Phil*, syndicated, December 16, 2003.
25. "Teen Sex: The Shocking Truth," *The Montel Williams Show*, January 27, 2005.
26. "Teen Sex: The Shocking Truth," *The Montel Williams Show*, January 27, 2005.
27. *American Morning*, CNN, July 5, 2005. Recall that *Seventeen* had in fact published one of the first articles that mentioned rainbow parties in 2003.
28. "Book Aimed at Teens Describes Sex Parties," *Hannity & Colmes*, Fox News, May 31, 2005.
29. "The Truth about Sex," *The Doctors*, May 27, 2010.
30. *The Today Show*, November 14, 2003; *Good Morning America*, May 26, 2004.
31. *News at 4:30 p.m.*, WHNT, channel 19 (Huntsville, AL), March 8, 2005.
32. *UPN 9 News*, WWOR, channel 9 (New York), November 6, 2006.
33. "Sk8tr Boyz," *George Lopez*, ABC, November 9, 2003.
34. "Lipstick on Your Panties," *Huff*, Showtime, November 1, 2004.
35. "Hooked," *Law & Order: Special Victims Unit*, NBC, February 1, 2005.
36. "Alex, Derek, and Gary," *Nip/Tuck*, F/X, October 5, 2005.
37. "Lipstick on Your Panties," *Huff*, Showtime, November 1, 2004.
38. "Consent," *Judging Amy*, CBS, October 26, 2004.
39. "Alex, Derek, and Gary," *Nip/Tuck*, F/X, October 5, 2005.
40. "Over the Rainbow," *The Hard Times of RJ Berger*, MTV, July 12, 2010. This episode is relevant to discussions in the news about whether some teens are trying to remain "technical virgins" by engaging in oral—or anal—sex, while avoiding vaginal penetration. Some people blame this mentality for the supposed "oral-sex epidemic" among teens.
41. *The Joy Behar Show*, CNN, April 10, 2010.
42. *The Today Show*, NBC, April 10, 2012.
43. "The Great Firewall," *The Good Wife*, CBS, March 1, 2010. There are other examples: an episode of *Degrassi: The Next Generation* ("Secret: Parts 1 & 2," CTV [Canada], November 30 and December 7, 2004) featured a plotline in which teens gave bracelets to their sexual partners; in an episode titled "Teen Sex," on *Penn &*

Teller: Bullshit! (Showtime, July 1, 2010), there is a close-up of black sex bracelets worn by one of the young women being interviewed.

44. *Saturday Night Live*, NBC, October 23, 2010.

45. Kingsbury (2008); *The Pregnancy Pact*, Lifetime, January 23, 2010.

NOTES TO CHAPTER 4

1. "Is Your Child Leading a Double Life?," *The Oprah Winfrey Show*, October 1, 2003; Pearce (2009).

2. Folklorists have long been aware that people disagree about the meanings of particular legends (Dégh and Vázsonyi 1973).

3. In most discussions, participants gave themselves code names; comments that seemed to have been signed with the author's true name have been attributed to "[name]."

4. partyboy, comment on Alex (2005), August 12, 2005.

5. claire, post on Jonesboro Forum (2008), January 23, 2010; ellipsis added.

6. zammara, post on Jonesboro Forum (2008), May 4, 2009.

7. auqagirl, comment on Alex (2005), April 13, 2009.

8. Anonymous, comment on Alex (2005), August 12, 2005.

9. looloo, post on Lifesupporters (2004), May 9, 2010.

10. Anonymous, post on Blurt It (2007), c. July 1, 2010.

11. yo momma, post on Jonesboro Forum (2008), September 21, 2008.

12. [name], comment on Alex (2005), August 12, 2005; ellipsis in original.

13. home slice, post on Jonesboro Forum (2008), November 26, 2008; ellipsis in original.

14. AsheeSweets, post on Lifesupporters (2004), March 16, 2009.

15. [name], post on Above Top Secret (2009), September 25, 2009; ellipsis in original.

16. ditto_n, post on NFBSK (2004), April 1, 2004.

17. tanta07, post on NFBSK (2004), June 17, 2004.

18. Brunvand (2001: 154–55).

19. aa*bn, post on Lifesupporters (2004), October 29, 2008; ellipsis added.

20. [name], comment on Lovepanky (2010), December 2, 2010.

21. Travis, comment on Alex (2005), August 25, 2005.

22. ash10107, post on TheDoctorsTV.com (2010), May 27, 2010.

23. Yo Don Vito, post on Jonesboro Forum (2008), September 21, 2008; ellipsis in original.

24. Lovepanky (2010); ellipsis in original.

25. Alex (2005).

26. me, comment on Worstall (2009), c. September 29, 2009; ellipsis in original.

27. Jade, post on Facebook (2008), c. October 1, 2009.

28. guest, post on Blurt It (2007), c. August 1, 2009.

29. guest, post on Blurt It (2007), c. August 1, 2009.

30. *Education Coffeehouse Newsletter* (2003).

31. stkatesgirl, post on TheDoctorsTV.com (2010), March 21, 2010; ellipsis added.

32. Shannon F., post on Talk San Francisco (2006), October 19, 2007.

33. sarasota, comment on Free Republic (2004), May 26, 2004. Our data do not contain any other reference to Oprah covering sex bracelets. Contemporary legends often incorporate erroneous claims about things that occurred on various talk shows (Brunvand 2001: 440–41).

34. Oualawouzou, post on NFBSK (2004), March 31, 2004; emphasis in original.

35. [name], post on Helium (2007), May 13, 2009. Folklorists use the term *ostension* to describe occasions when individuals act out a legend (Ellis 2001).

36. lalalla, post on Jonesboro Forum (2008), January 2, 2009.

37. AI386, "rainbow party," definition 25, *Urban Dictionary*, posted June 6, 2006, http://www.urbandictionary.com/define.php?term=rainbow+party&page=4 (retrieved December 30, 2013). Of course, the novel was published more than a year after the episode on *Oprah*.

38. lanna, post on Jonesboro Forum (2008), August 31, 2008.

39. adelaideparent, comment on PerthNow (2009), September 27, 2009.

40. Junior_G, comment on Free Republic (2004), May 26, 2004.

41. dontbestupid, "Rainbow party," definition 38, *Urban Dictionary*, posted July 30, 2005, http://www.urbandictionary.com/define.php?term=rainbow+party&page=6 (retrieved December 30, 2013). Giving oral sex to all the members of an athletic team is a motif found in some versions of the legend "The Promiscuous Cheerleader" (Fine 1992).

42. Miss Spider, "Rainbow Party," definition 27, *Urban Dictionary*, posted August 8, 2009, http://www.urbandictionary.com/define.php?term=rainbow+party&page=4 (retrieved December 30, 2013); ellipsis added.

43. Rubberbracelets.com (2010).

44. Jack of Perth, comment on PerthNow (2009), September 27, 2009.

45. jewbiegirl, comment on SparkNotes (2009), September 15, 2009.

46. AlienCarnage, post on Above Top Secret (2009), September 25, 2009.

47. KyoZero, post on Above Top Secret (2009), September 28, 2009.

48. dawniebrown, comment on Jen (2010), July 1, 2010. Several other posts on NFBSK (2004) offered similar recollections, including the explanation that "torture" meant an Indian burn.

49. [name], comment on Lovepanky (2010), January 4, 2010; ellipsis added.

50. Mark, comment on View from the Right (2004), May 25, 2004.

51. teenmom17, post on SteadyHealth (2006), December 1, 2009; ellipsis added, emphasis in original.

52. For example, see bobpage, post on Leatherneck.com (2004), May 27, 2004; montag813, comment on Free Republic (2004), May 26, 2004.

53. Tiffany "T-Liscious" W., post on Talk San Francisco (2006), February 22, 2006; ellipsis in original.

54. Duke, post on Lifesupporters (2004), September 12, 2009.

55. Coleus, comment on Free Republic (2004), May 26, 2004.

56. weci2i, post on NFBSK (2004), June 27, 2004.

57. AqueousBoy, comment on Alex (2005), August 12, 2005.

58. Chipper McGee, post on NFBSK (2004), July 31, 2005.

59. Agrippina, post on Straight Dope (2003), December 16, 2003.

60. [name], comment on Giarrusso (2010), January 29, 2010.

61. [name], comment on View from the Right (2004), May 26, 2004.

62. AqueousBoy, comment on Alex (2005), August 12, 2005.

63. pregpostmassage, comment on Conte (2009), September 16, 2009.

64. SparkNotes (2009).

65. Morrison's Lament, post on NFBSK (2004), March 31, 2004.

66. obama bin liner, "shag bands," definition 3, *Urban Dictionary*, posted July 15, 2009, http://www.urbandictionary.com/define.php?term=shag+bands (retrieved December 30, 2013).

67. Robyn, comment on PerthNow (2009), September 28, 2009.

68. Fenriz of Adelaide, comment on PerthNow (2009), September 28, 2009.

69. Cervaise, post on Straight Dope (2003), December 16, 2003.

70. MagoSA, post on Above Top Secret (2009), September 30, 2009.

71. Comment on Detentionslip.org (2009); ellipsis added, emphasis in original.

72. Smokin' Joe, comment on Free Republic (2004), May 27, 2009.

73. "and," comment on Worstall (2009), c. September 29, 2009.

74. Alex (2005).

75. [name], post on Helium (2007), December 7, 2007.

76. VRWCmember, comment on Free Republic (2004), May 26, 2004.

77. HairOfTheDog, comment on Free Republic (2004), May 26, 2004.

78. Flanagan (2006: 169).

79. Gemwolf (2012); ellipses in original.

80. Rogue1stclass, post on NFBSK (2004), June 15, 2004; ellipsis in original.

81. shorty_gurlie, comment on SparkNotes (2009), September 15, 2009.

82. ModelBreaker, comment on Free Republic (2004), May 26, 2004; ellipsis in original.

83. Gemwolf (2012); ellipsis in original.

84. [name], comment on Alex (2005), August 17, 2005.

85. JRDelirious, post on Straight Dope (2003), December 17, 2003.

86. [name], comment on Alex (2005), August 13, 2005.

87. partyboy, comment on Alex (2005), August 15, 2005.

88. [name], comment on View from the Right (2004), June 2, 2004.

89. Old Sarge, comment on Free Republic (2004), May 26, 2004.

90. Ben "Same As It Ever Was" P., post on Talk San Francisco (2006), October 19, 2007.

91. goodtwin91, comment on SparkNotes (2009), September 15, 2009.

92. TwilightFan, post on Lifesupporters (2004), October 11, 2009.

93. Ianna, post on Jonesboro Forum (2008), August 31, 2008.

94. Abby, post on Lifesupporters (2004), April 17, 2010.

95. xxteamovxx, post on Lifesupporters (2004), August 13, 2010.

96. [name], post on Helium (2007), December 10, 2007.

97. ag97, "rainbow party," definition 4, *Urban Dictionary*, posted March 14, 2005, http://www.urbandictionary.com/define.php?term=rainbow+party (retrieved December 30, 2013).

98. [name], post on Helium (2007), December 7, 2007.

99. Advicenators (2007).

100. -x-Jazz-x-, post on Blurt It (2007), c. August 1, 2007.

101. Got Milk, "rainbow party," definition 23, *Urban Dictionary*, posted November 23, 2005, http://www.urbandictionary.com/define.php?term=rainbow+party&page=4 (retrieved December 30, 2013).

102. [name], "rainbow party," definition 10, *Urban Dictionary*, posted September 9, 2005, http://www.urbandictionary.com/define.php?term=rainbow+party&page=2 (retrieved December 30, 2013).

103. geminilee, post on NFBSK (2009), November 11, 2009.

104. Proxidike, comment on SparkNotes (2009), September 16, 2009.

105. jamcat, comment on PerthNow (2009), September 27, 2009.

106. Moosi, comment on V. Miller (2009), c. September 10, 2009.

107. carbonware, post on *Education Blog* (2009), September 15, 2009.

108. *STOP Online Exploitation of Children and Teenagers's* [*sic*] *Blog* (2009), November 16, 2009.

109. Local 5-0, comment on M. Roberts (2009), March 24, 2010; ellipsis added.

110. Tasmin, post on Facebook (2008), c. 2008.

111. samantha, comment on Worstall (2009), c. September 29, 2009. While we did not find any news reports of violence related to sex bracelets in any English-speaking country, there were reports that a 13-year-old Brazilian girl had been pressured to have sex after a group of boys broke a bracelet. This story received global press coverage. In the days that followed, Brazilian authorities speculated that some murders might be linked to the bracelets because the victims were wearing them, and Brazil banned sex bracelets (Guanabee 2010).

112. juggalo77, post on Above Top Secret (2009), September 9, 2009.

NOTES TO CHAPTER 5

1. J. Irvine (2002); Luker (2006).

2. For one version of these claims, see Gardner (2011).

3. The first appearance in print of the term *sexting* seems to have been in a 2005 article in Australia's *Sunday Telegraph Magazine*. The article discussed cricket star Shane Warne's extramarital affairs, which included sexual text messages that had been obtained by the press (Roberts 2005).

4. Rogers (2008): Reitz (2008).

5. Associated Press (2008).
6. Jayson (2008).
7. These findings paralleled those from earlier surveys showing that 13%–19% of young people reported experiencing online "sexual solicitation" (defined broadly to include any request for sexual talk or sexual information), although relatively few of these messages troubled the teens who received them (Mitchell, Finkelhor, and Wolak 2001; Mitchell, Wolak, and Finkelhor 2008).
8. *The Today Show*, NBC, December 10, 2008.
9. *World News Tonight*, ABC, December 13, 2008.
10. *The Early Show*, CBS, January 15, 2009.
11. *The Today Show*, NBC, January 22, 2009.
12. Parker (2009).
13. Lithwick (2009).
14. Associated Press (2009).
15. *Good Morning America*, ABC, December 26, 2008.
16. *Newsroom*, CNN, February 9, 2011.
17. A Thin Line (2009).
18. Richards (2009).
19. Marte (2010).
20. Best (2013: 32).
21. Hamill (2009).
22. Celizic (2009).
23. *Nightline*, ABC, April 1, 2010.
24. *Nightline*, April 1, 2010.
25. *The Early Show*, CBS, March 24, 2010.
26. *Dr. Drew*, CNN, April 18, 2011.
27. *American Morning*, CNN, April 7, 2009.
28. Lenhart (2009).
29. Wolak and Finkelhor (2011: 1).
30. Harris (2006).
31. Center for Drug Evaluation and Research (1999).
32. Blumenthal (2007).
33. *Tell Me More*, NPR, May 10, 2007.
34. Landler (2011); Harris (2011). The administration eventually gave in to further protests, so the pill became available to all ages without a prescription (Shear and Belluck 2013).

NOTES TO CHAPTER 6

1. Hartmann (2011).
2. A survey by Laumann et al. (1994: 325) found that the average age at first intercourse among white respondents born 1933–42 (i.e., roughly the grandparents of today's teens) was 19 for females and 18 for males; among those born 1963–67

(i.e., roughly the parents of today's teens), the age was 18 for both sexes. African Americans had lower average ages, so the overall average was a bit lower than the figure for whites.

3. Martinez, Copen, and Abma (2011). It is important to appreciate the nature of averages across age categories. When the data show that, on average, 43% of females ages 15–19 have had sexual intercourse, the percentage of sexually experienced 15-year-olds is undoubtedly less than 43%, just as the percentage of 19-year-olds who have had sex will be higher than 43%.

4. Eaton et al. (2012).

5. Hawes, Wellings, and Stephenson (2010); Rotermann (2008); Rissel et al. (2003); Wellings et al. (2001).

6. Among Alfred Kinsey's youngest female respondents (born 1910–19) who married before they turned 21 and who had had premarital intercourse, 63% reported having premarital coitus with only one male (Kinsey et al., [1953] 1965: 336). Edward Laumann et al. (1994: 328) found that, over time, women reported somewhat more sexual partners as teens: over 90% of those born 1933–42 reported having had zero or only one partner before they turned 18; that percentage fell to about 64% for those born 1963–74.

7. U.S. Bureau of the Census (2011).

8. Martinez, Copen, and Abma (2011: 7). In Canada in 2005, 29% of 15- to 17-year-olds said they had had more than one sexual partner in the previous year (Rotermann 2008).

9. Eaton et al. (2012).

10. Flanagan (2006); Young (2006).

11. Hans, Gillen, and Akande (2010).

12. Copen, Chandra, and Martinez (2012: 10).

13. Chandra, Mosher, and Copen (2011). For Australian data on age at first experience with oral sex, see Rissel et al. (2003).

14. Regnerus and Uecker (2011).

15. Martinez, Copen, and Abma (2011).

16. Regnerus and Uecker (2011: 67).

17. Bogle (2008).

18. Boyce et al. (2006); Coleman and Testa (2008); Boyle et al. (2003). Only a tiny proportion—less than 3%—of British females report having had sex with someone they had just met (Wellings et al. 2001).

19. Wood (2012).

20. Walters (2004: 3H).

21. Nelson (2010).

22. *The Today Show*, NBC, November 14, 2003.

23. Nicholas (2009); emphasis in original.

24. Hennessy (2009: 17).

25. Lewin (2005: G1).

26. Wente (2004: A21).
27. *Pittsburgh Post-Gazette* (2004: N4).
28. Elliott (2012: 3). See also Schalet (2011).
29. "Girls Misbehaving," *Dr. Phil*, syndicated, December 16, 2003.
30. Meeker (2002); see also Liebau (2007).
31. Dalton (2010); Gross and Foster (2005).
32. American Psychological Association (2007: 2). See also Durham (2008); Levin and Kilbourne (2008); Liebau (2007); Olfman (2009).
33. D. Sherman (2008: A1).
34. *Sunday Territorian* (2009: 6).
35. *Tell Me More*, NPR, October 31, 2011.
36. West (2005: A21).
37. Gerald Augustinus, *The Cafeteria Is Closed* (defunct blog), quoted in Banerjee (2005).
38. Diaz (2009).
39. Meeker (2002: 18).
40. Singh, Darroch, and Frost (2001); Halpern and Haydon (2012).
41. Eaton et al. (2012).
42. Centers for Disease Control and Prevention (2009: 1).
43. Martinez, Copen, and Abma (2011).
44. Martinez, Copen, and Abma (2011).
45. Longmore et al. (2009).
46. Regnerus (2007).
47. Floyd and Latimer (2010).
48. Henderson (2010).

REFERENCES

Above Top Secret. 2009. "Children Being Encouraged to Engage in Sexual Practices?" Forum. First post September 24. http://www.abovetopsecret.com/forum/thread504272 (retrieved October 2, 2010).

Advicenators. 2007. "Jelly Bracelets." Q&A website. Question posted June 9. http://www.advicenators.com/qview.php?q=496334 (retrieved September 22, 2010).

Agrell, Siri. 2008. "Birds, Bees and Oral Sex." *Globe and Mail*, September 11.

Alex. 2005. "Rainbow Parties." Museum of Hoaxes, August 11. http://www.museumof hoaxes.com/hoax/weblog/comments/3524/P60/ (retrieved May 20, 2012).

Allport, Gordon W., and Leo Postman. 1947. *The Psychology of Rumor*. New York: Holt.

American Psychological Association. 2007. *Report of the APA Task Force on the Sexualization of Girls: Executive Summary*. Washington, DC: American Psychological Association.

Amyth.com. 2003. "Sex Bracelets and Their Color Meanings." http:www.amyth.com/Odd/Sex-Bracelets.html (retrieved September 1, 2010).

Associated Press. 2008. "Teen Sentenced for Sending Nude Cell Phone Photos." August 29.

———. 2009. "Prosecutors: Ohio Laws on Pornography Need Updating." March 5.

Bailey, Beth L. 1988. *From Front Porch to Back Seat: Courtship in Twentieth-Century America*. Baltimore: Johns Hopkins University Press.

———. 2004. "From Front Porch to Back Seat: A History of the Date." *OAH Magazine of History* 18 (July): 23–26.

Banerjee, Bidisha. 2005. "Non!" Slate.com, May 26. http://www.slate.com/articles/news_and_politics/todays_blogs/2005/05/non.html (retrieved October 15, 2012).

Barclay, Dorothy. 1960. "Social Life—Too Much Too Soon?" *New York Times Magazine*, April 24, 89.

BBC News. 2009. "MP Calls for 'Sex Bracelet' Ban." September 25. http://news.bbc .co.uk/2/hi/uk_news/england/west_yorkshire/8274178.stm (retrieved October 16, 2009).

Beisel, Nicola. 1997. *Imperiled Innocents: Anthony Comstock and Family Reproduction in Victorian America.* Princeton: Princeton University Press.

Beresin, Anna R. 2010. *Recess Battles: Playing, Fighting, and Storytelling.* Jackson: University Press of Mississippi.

Bernstein, Elizabeth. 2010. "Militarized Humanitarianism Meets Carceral Feminism: The Politics of Sex, Rights, and Freedom in Contemporary Antitrafficking Campaigns." *Signs* 36:45–71.

Berry, Jake. 2009. "Parents Face Cell Phone Dilemma for Teens." *Cape Cod Times,* March 1.

Best, Joel. 1990. *Threatened Children: Rhetoric and Concern about Child-Victims.* Chicago: University of Chicago Press.

———. 2013. *Social Problems.* 2nd ed. New York: Norton.

Blank, Trevor J., ed. 2009. *Folklore and the Internet: Vernacular Expression in a Digital World.* Logan: Utah State University Press.

Blumenthal, Ralph. 2007. "Texas Is First to Require Cancer Shots for Schoolgirls." *New York Times,* February 3, 9.

Blurt It. 2007. "What Are Shag Bands?" Q&A website. http://www.blurtit.com/q385436.html (retrieved September 15, 2010).

Bogle, Kathleen A. 2008. *Hooking Up: Sex, Dating, and Relationships on Campus.* New York: NYU Press.

Boyce, William, Maryanne Doherty-Poirier, Christian Fortin, Owen Gallupe, Matt King, and David MacKinnon. 2006. "Sexual Health of Canadian Youth: Findings from the Canadian Youth, Sexual Health and HIV/AIDS Study." *Canadian Journal of Human Sexuality* 15:59–68.

Boyle, Frances M., Michael P. Dunne, David M. Purdie, Jake M. Najman, and Michele D. Cook. 2003. "Early Patterns of Sexual Activity: Age Cohort Differences in Australia." *International Journal of STD and AIDS* 14:745–52.

Brown, Jane D., Jeanne R. Steele, and Kim Walsh-Childers, eds. 2002. *Sexual Teens, Sexual Media: Investigating Media's Influence on Adolescent Sexuality.* Mahwah, NJ: Lawrence Erlbaum.

Brunvand, Jan Harold. 1981. *The Vanishing Hitchhiker: American Urban Legends and Their Meanings.* New York: Norton.

———. 2001. *Encyclopedia of Urban Legends.* New York: Norton.

CafePress. 2010. "Jelly Bracelet Sex Code T-Shirt." http://www.cafepress.com/mf/3355977/jelly-bracelet-sex-code_tshirt?productId=23155908 (retrieved October 3, 2010).

Carlsson-Page, Nancy, and Diane E. Levin. 1990. *Who's Calling the Shots? How to Respond Effectively to Children's Fascination with War Play and War Toys.* Philadelphia: New Society.

Cawelti, John G. 1976. *Adventure, Mystery, and Romance: Formula Stories as Art and Popular Culture.* Chicago: University of Chicago Press.

Celizic, Mike. 2009. "Her Teen Committed Suicide over 'Sexting.'" Today Parenting,

March 6. http://today.msnbc.msn.com/id/29546030%20/ns/today-parenting_and_
family/t/her-teen-committed-suicide-over-sexting/#.ULKTymfheu8 (retrieved
October 15, 2012).

Center for Drug Evaluation and Research. 1999. Approval letter for Plan B. July 28.
http://web.archive.org/web/20070221131517/http://www.fda.gov/cder/foi/nda/99/
21-045_Plan%20B_Approv.pdf (retrieved January 15, 2013).

Centers of Disease Control and Prevention. 2009. *Sexually Transmitted Diseases in
the United States, 2008.* November. http://www.cdc.gov/std/stats08/trends.htm
(retrieved January 14, 2013).

Chandra, Anjani, William D. Mosher, and Casey Copen. 2011. "Sexual Behavior, Sexual
Attraction, and Sexual Identity in the United States: Data from the 2006–2008
National Survey of Family Growth." Centers for Disease Control, National Center
for Health Statistics. *National Health Statistics Reports* 36. http://www.cdc.gov/nchs/
data/nhsr/nhsr036.pdf (retrieved October 12, 2012).

Chapman, Brian. 2010. "Bracelets." *Legends & Rumors* (blog). http://legendsrumors
.blogspot.com/search/label/Bracelets (retrieved July 28, 2010).

Cohen, Stanley. (1972) 2002. *Folk Devils and Moral Panics.* 3rd ed. New York:
Routledge.

Coleman, Lester M., and Adrienne Testa. 2008. "Sexual Health Knowledge, Attitudes
and Behaviours: Variations among a Religiously Diverse Sample of Young People in
London, UK." *Ethnicity and Health* 13:55–72.

Conte, Kim. 2009. "Middle School Sex Bracelet Panic." The Stir, September 15. http://
thestir.cafemom.com/big_kid/7250/middle_school_sex_bracelet_panic?next=1
(retrieved October 4, 2010).

Copen, Casey E., Anjani Chandra, and Gladys Martinez. 2012. "Prevalence and Timing
of Oral Sex with Opposite-Sex Partners among Females and Males Aged 15–24."
Centers for Disease Control, National Center for Health Statistics. *National Health
Statistics Reports* 56. http://www.cdc.gov/nchs/data/nhsr/nhsr056.pdf (retrieved
October 12, 2012).

Dalton, Ryan. 2010. *Moved.* Central Milton Keynes, UK: AuthorHouse.

Dégh, Linda, and Andrew Vázsonyi. 1973. "The Dialectics of the Legend." Indiana University Folklore Preprint Series 1, no. 6. Bloomington: Indiana University Folklore
Institute.

D'Emilio, John, and Estelle B. Freedman. 1988. *Intimate Matters: A History of Sexuality
in America.* New York: Harper & Row.

Detentionslip.org. 2009. "Lafayette Middle School Discourages Jelly Bracelets, Citing Sexual Meanings." September. http://www.detentionslip.org/2009/09/lafayette
-middle-school-discourages.html (retrieved September 27, 2010).

Diaz, Missy. 2009. "In Florida, 'Sexting' Can Have Legal Consequences for Sender and
Receiver." *South Florida Sun-Sentinel*, July 29.

Downs, Anthony. 1972. "Up and Down with Ecology—The 'Issue-Attention Cycle.'"
Public Interest 28:38–50.

Downs, Donald Alexander. 1989. *The New Politics of Pornography*. Chicago: University of Chicago Press.

Dundes, Alan, and Carl R. Pagter. 1975. *Urban Folklore from the Paperwork Empire*. Austin, TX: American Folklore Society.

Durham, M. Gigi. 2008. *The Lolita Effect: The Media Sexualization of Young Girls and What We Can Do about It*. Woodstock, NY: Overlook.

Eaton, Danice K., Laura Kann, Steve Kinchen, Shari Shanklin, Katherine H. Flint, Joseph Hawkins, Williams A. Harris, et al. 2012. "Youth Risk Behavior Surveillance—United States, 2011." Centers for Disease Control and Prevention. *Surveillance Summaries* 61 (SSO4). http://www.cdc.gov/mmwr/preview/mmwrhtml/ss6104a1.htm (retrieved October 12, 2012).

Education Blog. 2009. "Colorado School Bans Bracelets Used in Sex Game." *South Florida Sun-Sentinel*, September 14. http://weblogs.sun-sentinel.com/education blog/2009/09/colorado_school-bans-bracelets-used-in-sex-game.html (retrieved October 6, 2010).

Education Coffeehouse Newsletter. 2003. "A Warning for Parents: Jelly Bracelets." November.

Elliott, Sinikka. 2010. "Parents' Constructions of Teen Sexuality: Sex Panics, Contradictory Discourses, and Social Inequality." *Symbolic Interaction* 33:191–212.

———. 2012. *Not My Kid: What Parents Believe about the Sex Lives of Their Teenagers*. New York: NYU Press.

Ellis, Bill. 1991. "The Last Thing Said: The *Challenger* Disaster Jokes and Closure." *International Folklore Review* 8:110–24.

———. 1994. " 'The Hook' Reconsidered: Problems in Classifying and Interpreting Adolescent Horror Legends." *Folklore* 105:61–75.

———. 2001. *Aliens, Ghosts, and Cults: Legends We Live*. Jackson: University Press of Mississippi.

———. 2003. "Making a Big Apple Crumble: The Role of Humor in Constructing a Global Response to Disaster." In *Of Corpse: Death and Humor in Folklore and Popular Culture*, edited by Peter Narváez, 35–79. Logan: Utah State University Press.

Epstein, Debbie. 1999. "Sex Play: Romantic Significations, Sexism and Silences in the Schoolyard." In *A Dangerous Knowing: Sexuality, Pedagogy and Popular Culture*, edited by Debbie Epstein and James T. Sears, 25–42. New York: Cassell.

Facebook. 2008. "Means of Colors." http://www.facebook.com/pages/shag-bands/219260375704#!/topic.php?uid=219260375704&topic=14633 (retrieved October 1, 2010).

Fass, Paula S. 1977. *The Damned and the Beautiful: American Youth in the 1920's*. New York: Oxford University Press.

Ferguson, Ann Arnett. 2000. *Bad Boys: Public Schools in the Making of Black Masculinity*. Ann Arbor: University of Michigan Press.

Fields, Jessica. 2005. " 'Children Having Children': Race, Innocence, and Sexuality Education." *Social Problems* 52:549–71.

Fine, Gary Alan. 1992. *Manufacturing Tales: Sex and Money in Contemporary Legends.* Knoxville: University of Tennessee Press.

Fine, Gary Alan, Véronique Campion-Vincent, and Chip Heath, eds. 2005. *Rumor Mills: The Social Impact of Rumor and Legend.* New Brunswick, NJ: Aldine-Transaction.

Fine, Gary Alan, and Bill Ellis. 2010. *The Global Grapevine: Why Rumors of Terrorism, Immigration, and Trade Matter.* New York: Oxford University Press.

Fine, Gary Alan, Beth Montemurro, Bonnie Semora, Marybeth C. Stalp, Dane S. Claussen, and Zayda Sierra. 1998. "Social Order through a Prism: Color as Collective Representation." *Sociological Inquiry* 68:443–57.

Fine, Gary Alan, and Patricia A. Turner. 2001. *Whispers on the Color Line: Rumor and Race in America.* Berkeley: University of California Press.

Flanagan, Caitlin. 2006. "Are You There God? It's Me, Monica." *Atlantic Monthly*, January–February, 167–74, 176–80, 182.

Floyd, Leah J., and William Latimer. 2010. "Adolescent Sexual Behaviors at Varying Levels of Substance Use Frequency." *Journal of Child and Adolescent Substance Abuse* 19:66–77.

Free Republic. 2004. "Kids Wearing Rubber 'Sex Bracelets.'" May 26. http://www.free republic.com/focus/f-backroom/1142544/posts#comment (retrieved September 29, 2010).

Furedi, Frank. 2001. *Paranoid Parenting: Abandon Your Anxieties and Be a Good Parent.* London: Penguin.

Gardner, Christine J. 2011. *Making Chastity Sexy: The Rhetoric of Evangelical Abstinence Campaigns.* Berkeley: University of California Press.

Garvey, Marianne, and Carl Campanile. 2004. "Kids' Cuff Kink: Raunchy 'Sex Bracelet' Fad Hits City Schools." *New York Post*, May 23, 5.

Gay City USA. 2011. "Gay Hanky Codes." http://www.gaycityusa.com/hankycodes.htm (retrieved June 7, 2011).

Gemwolf. 2012. "Rainbow Parties—Fantasy, Myth or Reality?" *A Day in the Life of the Gemwolf* (blog), January 23. http://thegemwolf.blogspot.com/2012/01/rainbow-parties-fantasy-myth-or-reality.html?zx=14d71c7e0e0a8c20 (retrieved May 25, 2012).

Giarrusso, Theresa Walsh. 2010. "Teen Trend: Does Her Bracelet Mean Something Sexual?" *Momania* (blog), *Atlanta Journal-Constitution*, January 29. http://blogs.ajc .com/momania/2010/01/29/teen-trenddoes-her-bracelet-mean-something-sexual/ (retrieved September 29, 2010).

Gitlin, Todd. 1983. *Inside Prime Time.* New York: Pantheon.

Goode, Erich, and Nachman Ben-Yehuda. 2009. *Moral Panics: The Social Construction of Deviance.* 2nd ed. New York: Wiley-Blackwell.

Gregory, Katherine. 2010. "Confessions of At-Risk Teens: Abstinence, the Social Construction of Promiscuity, and *The Oprah Winfrey Show*." In *Stories of Oprah: The Oprahfication of American Culture*, edited by Trystan T. Cotten and Kimberly Springer, 85–98. Jackson: University Press of Mississippi.

Grineski, Steve. 1996. *Cooperative Learning in Physical Education*. Champaign, IL: Human Kinetics.

Gross, Craig, and Mike Foster. 2005. *Questions You Can't Ask Your Mama about Sex*. Grand Rapids, MI: Zondervan.

Guanabee. 2010. "Brazil Bans Sex Bracelets after Two Murders and a Rape." April 9. http://guanabee.com/2010/04/sex-bracelets (retrieved September 16, 2010).

Halpern, Carolyn Tucker, and Abigail A. Haydon. 2012. "Sexual Timetables for Oral-Genital, Vaginal, and Anal Intercourse: Sociodemographic Comparisons in a Nationally Representative Sample of Adolescents." *American Journal of Public Health* 102:1221–28.

Hamill, Sean D. 2009. "Students Sue Prosecutor in Cellphone Photos Case." *New York Times*, March 26, 21.

Hans, Jason D., Martie Gillen, and Katrina Akande. 2010. "Sex Redefined: The Reclassification of Oral-Genital Contact." *Perspectives on Sexual and Reproductive Health* 42:74–78.

Harris, Gardiner. 2006. "U.S. Approves Use of Vaccine for Cervical Cancer." *New York Times*, June 8, A1.

———. 2011. "Plan to Widen Availability of Morning-After Pill Is Rejected." *New York Times*, December 7.

Hartmann, Margaret. 2011. "Group Sex Is the Latest Disturbing Teen Trend." Jezebel .com, December 18. http://jezebel.com/5869215/group-sex-is-the-latest-disturbing-teen-trend (retrieved December 19, 2011).

Hawes, Zoé Coline, Kaye Wellings, and Judith Stephenson. 2010. "First Heterosexual Intercourse in the United Kingdom: A Review of the Literature." *Journal of Sex Research* 47:137–52.

Heath, Chip, Chris Bell, and Emily Sternberg. 2001. "Emotional Selection in Memes: The Case of Urban Legends." *Journal of Personality and Social Psychology* 81: 1028–41.

Helium. 2007. "Jelly Bracelets: An Invitation to Sex?" Forum. http://www.helium.com/items/1447814-jelly-bracelets-sex? (retrieved October 2, 2010).

Henderson, J. Maureen. 2010. "Of Spice Sniffing and Neck Biting." True/Slant, July 8. http://trueslant.com/jmaureenhenderson/2010/07/08/of-spice-sniffing-and-neck-biting/ (retrieved October 14, 2012).

Hennessy, Carly. 2009. "They're Called 'Shag Bands' and They Are . . . a Parent's Worst Nightmare." *Sunday Mail* (Australia), September 27, 17.

Herdt, Gilbert, ed. 2009. *Moral Panics, Sex Panics: Fear and the Fight over Sexual Rights*. New York: NYU Press.

Hier, Sean. ed. 2011. *Moral Panic and the Politics of Anxiety*. New York: Routledge.

Hill, Jennifer D. 2010. "The Teen Sexting Dilemma: A Look at How Teen Sexting Has Been Treated in the Criminal Justice System and Suggested Responses for Arizona." *Phoenix Law Review* 4:561–601.

Hine, Christine. 2000. *Virtual Ethnography*. Thousand Oaks, CA: Sage.

———, ed. 2005. *Virtual Methods: Issues in Social Research on the Internet.* Oxford, UK: Berg.

Howey, Noelle. 2003. "Oral Report." *Seventeen,* August, 218–21.

Irvine, Janice M. 2002. *Talk about Sex: The Battles over Sex Education in the United States.* Berkeley: University of California Press.

———. 2006. "Emotional Scripts of Sex Panics." *Sexuality Research and Social Policy* 3: 82–94.

Irvine, Martha. 2003. " 'Sex What?': Controversy Surrounds Popular Bracelets, but Some Say It's Hype." Associated Press, December 10.

Jayson, Sharon. 2008. "In Tech Flirting, Decorum Optional: Racy Pics, Messages Flying among Young." *USA Today,* December 10, 1A.

Jen. 2010. " 'Shag Bands' and Other Scary 'Children's Games'!" *The King and Eye* (blog), July 1. http://www.thekingandeye.com/2010/07/shag-bands-and-other-scary -childrens.html (retrieved September 28, 2010).

Jenkins, Philip. 1998. *Moral Panic: Changing Concepts of the Child Molester in Modern America.* New Haven: Yale University Press.

———. 2006. *Decade of Nightmares: The End of the Sixties and the Making of Eighties America.* New York: Oxford University Press.

Jonesboro Forum. 2008. "Sex Bracelets." Topix forum. http://www.topix.com/forum/ city/jonesboro-ar/TLK0EP623BEC85oEO (retrieved October 3, 2010).

Kincaid, James R. 1998. *Erotic Innocence: The Culture of Child Molesting.* Durham: Duke University Press.

Kingsbury, Kathleen. 2008. "Pregnancy Boom at Gloucester High." *Time,* June 18.

Kinsey, Alfred C., Wardell B. Pomeroy, Clyde E. Martin, and Paul H. Gebhard. (1953) 1965. *Sexual Behavior in the Human Female.* New York: Pocket Books.

Kliff, Sarah. 2013. "Most Americans Think Teen Pregnancy Is Getting Worse. Most Americans Are Wrong." *Washington Post,* April 1. http://www.washingtonpost.com/ blogs/wonkblog/wp/2013/04/01/most-americans-think-teen-pregnancy-is-getting -worse-most-americans-are-wrong/ (retrieved October 17, 2013).

Krinsky, Charles, ed. 2013. *The Ashgate Research Companion to Moral Panics.* Burling- ton, VT: Ashgate.

Kurti, Lazlo. 1988. "The Politics of Joking: Popular Response to Chernobyl." *Journal of American Folklore* 101:324–34.

Lancaster, Roger N. 2011. *Sex Panic and the Punitive State.* Berkeley: University of Cali- fornia Press.

Landler, Mark. 2011. "Obama Backs Limit on Sale to Teenagers of Morning-After Pill." *New York Times,* December 9.

Langlois, Janet. 1983. "The Belle Isle Bridge Incident: Legend, Dialectic and Semiotic System in the 1943 Detroit Race Riots." *Journal of American Folklore* 96:183–96.

Laumann, Edward O., John H. Gagnon, Robert T. Michael, and Stuart Michaels. 1994. *The Social Organization of Sexuality: Sexual Practices in the United States.* Chicago: University of Chicago Press.

Leatherneck.com. 2004. "Kids Wearing Rubber 'Sex Bracelets.'" Forum. First post May 27. http://www.leatherneck.com/forums/archive/index.php/t-14840.html (retrieved October 2, 2010).

Lenhart, Amanda. 2009. "Teens and Sexting." Pew Research Center. December 15. http://pewinternet.org/Reports/2009/Teens-and-Sexting.aspx (retrieved October 1, 2012).

Leon, Chrysanthi S. 2011. *Sex Fiends, Perverts, and Pedophiles: Understanding Sex Crime Policy in America.* New York: NYU Press.

Letukas, Lynn. 2012. "The Ascent of Punditry: Media and the Construction of Cable News." Ph.D. diss., University of Delaware.

Levin, Diane E., and Jean Kilbourne. 2008. *So Sexy So Soon: The New Sexualized Childhood and What Parents Can Do to Protect Their Kids.* New York: Ballantine.

Levy, Ariel. 2005. *Female Chauvinist Pigs: Women and the Rise of Raunch Culture.* New York: Free Press.

Lewin, Tamar. 2005. "Are These Parties for Real?" *New York Times,* June 30, G1.

Lexington Forum. 2010. "Sex Bracelets." Topix forum. First post June 2. http://www .topix.com/forum/city/lexington-ky/TQ2LAD830OQ7V2P08 (retrieved November 29, 2012).

Liebau, Carol Platt. 2007. *Prude: How the Sex-Obsessed Culture Damages Girls (and America, Too!).* New York: Center Street.

Lifesupporters. 2004. "Jelly Bracelets?! What Do They Mean." General Discussion forum. First post October 23. http://www.lifesupporters.com/forums/general -discussion/jelly-bracelets-what-do-they-mean-283.html (retrieved September 25, 2010)

Lithwick, Dahlia. 2009. "Teens, Nude Photos, and the Law." *Newsweek,* February 23, 18.

Longmore, Monica A., Abbey L. Eng, Peggy C. Giordano, and Wendy D. Manning. 2009. "Parenting and Adolescents' Sexual Initiation." *Journal of Marriage and Family* 71:969–82.

Lovepanky. 2010. "Rainbow Party—The Dark Secrets of Rainbow Parties." http://www .lovepanky.com/sensual-tease/obsession/rainbow-party (retrieved May 20, 2012).

Lowney, Kathleen S. 1999. *Baring Our Souls: TV Talk Shows and the Religion of Recovery.* Hawthorne, NY: Aldine de Gruyter.

Lowney, Kathleen S., and Joel Best. 1996. "What Waco Stood For: Jokes as Popular Constructions of Social Problems." *Perspectives on Social Problems* 8:77–98.

Luker, Kristin. 2006. *When Sex Goes to School: Warring Views on Sex—and Sex Education—since the Sixties.* New York: Norton.

MacGregor, Robert. 2012. "Chocolate as an Aphrodisiac: Are Green M&M's Randy Candy?" *Contemporary Legend,* 3rd series, 2:44–56.

Males, Mike A. 2010. *Teenage Sex and Pregnancy: Modern Myths, Unsexy Realities.* Santa Barbara, CA: Praeger.

Malkin, Michelle. 2005. "'Educational' Smut for Kids." *JWR Insight,* May 25. http:// www.jewishworldreview.com/michelle/malkin052505.php3 (retrieved July 16, 2012).

Malón, Agustin. 2011. "The 'Participating Victim' in the Study of Erotic Experiences between Children and Adults: An Historical Analysis." *Archives of Sexual Behavior* 40:169–88.

Marte, Jonnelle. 2010. "Anti-Sexting Campaigns Heat Up." *Wall Street Journal*, January 13.

Martin, Linda, and Kerry Segrave. 1988. *Anti-Rock: The Opposition to Rock and Roll.* Hamden, CT: Archon.

Martinez, Gladys, Casey E. Copen, and Joyce C. Abma. 2011. "Teenagers in the United States: Sexual Activity, Contraceptive Use, and Childbearing, 2006–2010 National Survey of Family Growth." Centers for Disease Control and Prevention, National Center for Health Statistics, *Vital and Health Statistics* 23 (31). http://www.cdc.gov/nchs/data/series/sr_23/sr23_031.pdf (retrieved October 12, 2012).

Maurer, D. W. 1976. "Language and the Sex Revolution: World War I through World War II." *American Speech* 51:5–24.

Meeker, Meg. 2002. *Epidemic: How Teen Sex Is Killing Our Kids.* Washington, DC: LifeLine.

Miller, Jody. 2008. *Getting Played: African American Girls, Urban Inequality, and Gendered Violence.* New York: NYU Press.

Miller, Vanessa. 2009. "Lafayette Middle School Discourages Jelly Bracelets, Citing Sexual Meanings." (*Boulder*) *Daily Camera* online, September 10. http://www.dailycamera.com/news/ci_13312346 (retrieved September 26, 2010).

Mitchell, Kimberly J., David Finkelhor, and Janis Wolak. 2001. "Risk Factors for and Impact of Online Sexual Solicitation of Youth." *Journal of the American Medical Association* 285 (June 20): 3011–14.

Mitchell, Kimberly J., Janis Wolak, and David Finkelhor. 2008. "Are Blogs Putting Youth at Risk for Online Sexual Solicitation or Harassment?" *Child Abuse and Neglect* 32:277–94.

momlogic. 2008. "Mom Logic Talks with Moms about Teen Sex 'Rainbow Parties.'" YouTube, March 28. http://www.youtube.com/watch?v=6TAe4FpEhU8 (retrieved July 15, 2012).

Murnen, Sarah. K., and Linda Smolak. 2000. "The Experience of Sexual Harassment among Grade School Students: Early Socialization or Female Subordination?" *Sex Roles* 43:1–17.

Nelson, Margaret K. 2010. *Parenting Out of Control: Anxious Parents in Uncertain Times.* New York: NYU Press.

Newall, Venetia. 1986. "Folklore and Male Homosexuality." *Folklore* 97:123–47.

New York Times. 1922. "Mothers Complain That Modern Girls 'Vamp' Their Sons at Petting Parties." February 22, 1.

NFBSK (Not for British School Kids). 2004. "Rainbow Parties?" Snopes.com message board. First post March 31. http://msgboard.snopes.com/cgi-bin/ultimatebb.cgi?ubb=print_topic;f=93;t=000821 (retrieved May 17, 2012).

———. 2009. "Sex Bracelets." Snopes.com message board. First post September 24.

http://message.snopes.com/showthread.php?t=51321 (retrieved September 30, 2010).

Nicholas, Sadie. 2009. "Thousands of Young Children Are Buying These Coloured Wristbands Every Week. But Parents Have No Idea of Their True Disturbing Meaning." *Daily Mail* (London), September 24.

Olfman, Sharna, ed. 2009. *The Sexualization of Childhood*. Westport, CT: Praeger.

Opie, Iona, and Peter Opie. 1959. *The Lore and Language of Schoolchildren*. Oxford, UK: Clarendon.

Parker, Elisabeth. 2009. "Sexting Can Be Trap for Teens." *St. Petersburg Times*, February 22, 1B.

Partridge, Eric. 1970. *A Dictionary of Slang and Unconventional English*. 7th ed. New York: Macmillan.

Pearce, Dulcie. 2009. "Bracelet Which Means Your Child Is Having SEX." *Sun* (UK), September 29, 34–35.

PerthNow. 2009. "Sexual Dangers in Child 'Shag Bands.'" September 27. http://www.perthnow.com.au/news/sexual-dangers-in-child-shag-bands/story-e6frg12c-1225780077066 (retrieved September 27, 2010).

Picoult, Jodi. 2006. *The Tenth Circle*. New York: Atria.

Pittsburgh Post-Gazette. 2004. "Suspect Symbolism: When Schooling Young Adults, Shouldn't Message Be Consistent?" June 9, N4.

Radway, Janice A. *Reading the Romance: Women, Patriarchy, and Popular Literature*. Chapel Hill: University of North Carolina Press.

Regnerus, Mark D. 2007. *Forbidden Fruit: Sex and Religion in the Lives of American Teenagers*. Oxford: Oxford University Press.

Regnerus, Mark D., and Jeremy Uecker. 2011. *Premarital Sex in America: How Young Americans Meet, Mate, and Think about Marrying*. New York: Oxford University Press.

Reitz, Stephanie. 2008. "Teens Are Sending Nude Photos via Cell Phone." Associated Press, June 4.

Renold, Emma. 2002. "Presumed Innocence: (Hetero)Sexual, Heterosexist and Homophobic Harassment among Primary School Girls and Boys." *Childhood* 9:415–34.

Ressner, Jeffrey. 2003. "Parents: Brace Yourselves." *Time*, October 27, 80.

Richards, Erin. 2009. "United Way Launches 'Safe Text' Billboard Campaign." *Journal Sentinel* (Milwaukee), March 4.

Rissel, Chris E., Juliet Richters, Andrew W. Grulich, Richard O. De Visser, and Anthony M. A. Smith. 2003. "First Experiences of Vaginal Intercourse and Oral Sex among a Representative Sample of Adults." *Australian and New Zealand Journal of Public Health* 27:131–37.

Roberts, Michael. 2009. "Meanings of Banned Jelly Bracelets: Is Silver a Hand Job, Fisting or Outdoor Sex?" *Latest Word* (blog), September 11. http://blogs.westword.com/latestword/2009/09/meanings_of_banned_jelly_brace.php (retrieved October 1, 2010).

Roberts, Yvonne. 2005. "The One and Only." *Sunday Telegraph Magazine* (Sydney, Australia), July 31, 22.

Rogers, Melinda. 2008. "Authorities Alarmed by Trend of Teens Sending Nude Photos via Cell Phone." *Salt Lake Tribune*, March 31.

Rosnow, Ralph L., and Gary Alan Fine. 1976. *Rumor and Gossip: The Social Psychology of Hearsay*. New York: Elsevier.

Rotermann, Michelle. 2008. "Trends in Teen Sexual Behaviour and Condom Use." *Statistics Canada Health Reports* 19 (September). http://www.statcan.gc.ca/pub/82 -003-x/2008003/article/10664-eng.pdf (retrieved October 13, 2012).

Roud, Steve. 2010. *The Lore of the Playground*. London: Random House.

Rubberbracelets.com. 2010. "Sex Bracelets and Their Meaning." http://rubberbracelets .com/articles/sex-bracelets-and-their-meaning/ (retrieved September 25, 2010).

Ruditis, Paul. 2005. *Rainbow Party*. New York: Simon Pulse.

Sax, Leonard. 2005. *Why Gender Matters: What Parents and Teachers Need to Know about the Emerging Science of Sex Differences*. New York: Broadway Books.

Schalet, Amy T. 2011. *Not under My Roof: Parents, Teens, and the Culture of Sex*. Chicago: University of Chicago Press.

Schudson, Michael. 2011. *The Sociology of the News*. 2nd ed. New York: Norton.

Schulte, Brigid. 2008. "For Little Children, Grown-Up Labels as Sexual Harassers." *Washington Post*, April 3, A1.

Sex-bracelets.com. 2009. "Sex Bracelets Color Code." http://www.sex-bracelets.com/ color.shtml (retrieved July 30, 2010).

Shear, Michael D., and Pam Belluck. 2013. "U.S. Drops Bid to Limit Sales of Morning-After Pill." *New York Times*, June 10.

Sheidlower, Jesse, ed. 2009. *The F-Word*. 3rd ed. New York: Oxford University Press.

Sherman, David. 2008. "Students Crumbling under Pressure." *Gazette* (Montreal), February 10, A1.

Sherman, Megan. 2011. "Sixteen, Sexting, and a Sex Offender: How Advances in Cell Phone Technology Have Led to Teenage Sex Offenders." *Boston University Journal of Science and Technology Law* 17:138–59.

Singh, Susheela, Jacqueline E. Darroch, and Jennifer J. Frost. 2001. "Socioeconomic Disadvantage and Adolescent Women's Sexual and Reproductive Behavior: The Case of Five Developed Countries." *Family Planning Perspectives* 33:251–58, 289.

SparkNotes. 2009. "Give Us the Sex Bracelets, Brittany!" September 15. http:// community.sparknotes.com/2009/09/15/give-us-the-sex-bracelets-brittany (retrieved October 2, 2010).

SteadyHealth. 2006. "Jelly Bracelets." Forum. First post August 23. http://www .steadyhealth.com/Jelly_Bracelets_t80182.html#820777 (retrieved September 28, 2010).

Stepp, Laura Sessions. 2004. "Threat Level Pink." *Washington Post*, January 5, C1.

STOP Online Exploitation of Children and Teenagers's [sic] Blog. 2009. "Do you Know What a 'Shag Band' Is . . . and Are your Children Wearing Them?" October 2.

http://www.myspace.com/stoponlineexploitation/blog/512640117 (retrieved September 29, 2010).

Straight Dope. 2003. "Sex Bracelets???" Message board. December 16. http://boards.straightdope.com/sdmb/showthread.php?t=229688 (retrieved October 5, 2010).

Sunday Territorian (Australia). 2009. "Schools Asked to Ban Sex Game." October 18, 6.

Sutton-Smith, Brian. 1959. "The Kissing Games of Adolescents in Ohio." *Midwest Folklore* 9:189–211.

———. 1972. *The Folkgames of Children*. Austin: University of Texas Press.

Talk San Francisco. 2006. "Kids and Sex Bracelets." Yelp forum. First post February 22. http://www.yelp.com/topic/san-francisco-kids-and-sex-bracelets (retrieved October 3, 2010).

TheDoctorsTV.com. 2010. "There Are Rainbow Parties??" Forum: "May 27, 2010—The Truth about Sex." First post February 22. http://www.thedoctorstv.com/forums/316-May-27-2-1-The-Truth-about-Sex/topics/6255-There-are-rainbow-parties (retrieved May 25, 2012).

Thin Line, A. 2009. "Sexting: What Is It?" http://www.athinline.org/facts/sexting (retrieved September 14, 2012).

Thorne, Barrie. 1993. *Gender Play: Girls and Boys in School*. New Brunswick: Rutgers University Press.

Tucker, Elizabeth. 2008. *Children's Folklore: A Handbook*. Westport, CT: Greenwood.

Urbina, Ian. 2009. "It's a Fork, It's a Spoon, It's a . . . Weapon?" *New York Times*, October 11. http://www.nytimes.com/2009/10/12/education/12discipline.html (retrieved October 15, 2011).

U.S. Bureau of the Census. 2011. "Estimated Median Age at First Marriage, by Sex: 1890 to the Present." http://www.census.gov/population/socdemo/hh-fam/ms2.csv (retrieved October 12, 2012).

View from the Right. 2004. "Girls in NYC Public Schools in Kinky Sex Games." May 24. http://www.amnation.com/vfr/archives/002317.html (retrieved September 27, 2010).

Walters, Lucie. 2004. "Teens, Voting Privilege Exacted a High Price." *Sunday Advocate* (Baton Rouge, LA), September 26, 3H.

Weaver, Sonja. 2005. "From Bracelets to Blowjobs: The Ideological Representation of Childhood Sexuality in the Media." *McMaster Journal of Communication* 2:35–49.

Weill, Sabrina. 2005. *The Real Truth about Teens and Sex*. New York: Perigee.

Wellings, Kaye, Kiran Nanchahal, Wendy Macdowall, Sally McManus, Bob Erens, Catherine H. Mercer, Anne M. Johnson, et al. 2001. "Sexual Behaviour in Britain: Early Heterosexual Experience." *Lancet* 358:1843–50.

Wells, Jennifer. 2004. "Softly, Now—First Impressions Are So Important." *Toronto Star*, February 7, K1.

Wente, Margaret. 2004. "Schoolgirls Want to Be the Sexiest Boy-Toy on the Block. Why?" *Globe and Mail*, February 10, A21.

West, Diana. 2005. "Lost in the City." *Washington Times*, June 3, A21.

Whatley, Mariamne H., and Elissa R. Henken. 2000. *Did You Hear about the Girl Who . . . ? Contemporary Legends, Folklore, and Human Sexuality.* New York: NYU Press.

Whitbread, Jane. 1957. "The Case for Going Steady." *New York Times*, July 14, 166.

Whiting, B. J. 1945. "Canoodle." *American Speech* 20:178–83.

Williams, Neil F. 1994. "The Physical Education Hall of Shame." *Journal of Physical Education, Recreation and Dance* 65 (February): 17–20.

Wolak, Janis, and David Finkelhor. 2011. "Sexting: A Typology." Crimes Against Children Research Center. March. http://www.unh.edu/ccrc/pdf/CV231_Sexting%20Typology%20Bulletin_4-6-11_revised.pdf (retrieved October 3, 2012).

Wolfe, Tom. 2000. *Hooking Up.* New York: Farrar, Straus and Giroux.

Wood, Steve. 2012. "Relationship Status on Social Network Offers Intimacy Barometer." *USA Today*, March 13.

Worstall, Tim. 2009. "Shag Bands and Rainbow Parties." Examiner.com, September 29. http://www.examiner.com/article/shag-bands-and-rainbow-parties (retrieved September 26, 2010).

Young, Cathy. 2006. "The Great Fellatio Scare." *Reason*, May, 18–20.

INDEX

Believers, 71–99
Beneficiaries of promoting concerns about teen sex, 131–137

Class, viii, x, 10–11, 49, 141–144
Colors of sex bracelets, meanings of, 37–40, 51, 61–63, 145n4, 150n31
Conservatives, sexual, 102, 120, 136, 139–140
Contemporary legends, 2, 14–16, 21–44, 47, 50, 69–72, 76, 96–98, 113, 132; Internet and, 23, 25–27, 69–99; media and, 23, 25–26; spread, 40–41, 44
Criminal penalties for sexting, 107–109, 112, 115, 119

Drama, television, 30, 32, 59–64

Evidence, 89–91

Facticity in television coverage, 50–52, 59, 64
Family characteristics, 143–44
Family values, 139–140
Fear, adults', vii, x, 93–94, 123–124, 143
Firsthand reports, 73–76
FOAF (friend of a friend), 76
Folklorists, 6, 13–14, 21–24, 31, 42, 44, 69–71, 147n32, 147n2
Formulas in popular culture, 46–47

Gardasil, 119–120
Gender, 10, 32
Genres in popular culture, 46–47
Girls, viii–ix, 4–5, 7, 10–12, 49, 53–54, 63–65, 110–111, 116, 121, 133, 137–139. See also Gender
Going steady, 7
Golliwogs, 145n4
Guests on television shows, 52–58

Infotainment, ix–x, 136

Jelly, 145n3
Joke cycles, 147n8

Kissing games, 6–7

Liberals, sexual, 102, 119–120, 136–137
Local television coverage, 58–59

Marketing sex bracelets, 81–82
Marriage, age at, 127
Media, viii–xi, 25, 29–36, 41–44, 79–81, 136–137
Methods of research, 10, 25–27, 148n10, 150n31
Myths, 147n32, 147n2

Online conversations, 69–99
Oprah Winfrey Show (on rainbow parties), 3, 28–32, 52, 125, 154n33
Oral sex among teens, 3–4, 49, 128–129
Ostension, 154n35

Panics, 17
Petting parties, 7
Plan B, 119–120
Playgrounds, 13–14
Plausibility, 87–89
Popular culture, corrupting effects of, viii, 8, 10, 12–13
Pragmatic stance toward youth sexuality, 9, 11, 102
Pregnancy pacts, 67
Probabilities, 87–89
Protective stance toward youth sexuality, 9–11, 102
Public opinion, 95

Race, viii, ix, 8, 10–11, 49, 141–144, 150n30
Rainbow parties, 3–4, 27–33; Internet and, 30–31, 73–99; media and, 28–33, 42, 133;

Joel Best is Professor of Sociology & Criminal Justice at the University of Delaware. He has published more than 20 books on social problems and deviance, including *Threatened Children, Random Violence, Damned Lies and Statistics,* and *The Student Loan Mess* (with Eric Best).

Kathleen A. Bogle is Associate Professor of Sociology and Criminal Justice at LaSalle University. She is the author of *Hooking Up: Sex, Dating, and Relationships on Campus,* also published by NYU Press.